My Name Was Alec
A Memoir

Allen Jacoby

Table of Contents

1. My Name Was Alec 7
2. Behind Barbed Wire...Again 9
3. Finally Home 13
4. A Part of Something 15
5. A New Name 18
6. A Word About Manhood 23
7. My Secret Identity 25
8. Belonging 28
9. Heroes 32
10. Get Out Jew! 35
11. Pop 37
12. I'm in the Army Now 40
13. Becoming a Paratrooper 46
14. Getting My Wings 50
15. A Job Well Done 52
16. The Academy 56
17. Graduation 60
18. Israel's Superheroes 64
19. The Tent 66

Table of Contents

20. Mission for Rivka 68
21. The Defenders 71
22. Rewards 74
23. The Old Man 77
24. Extra-Curricular Activities 80
25. When in Rome 85
26. More Family History 89
27. My Purpose 94
28. Conundrum 96
29. Israel's Bar Mitzvah 98
30. Revenge Interruptus 102
31. The Best Therapy 107
32. Talfiq 109
33. Mourning 114
34. The Value of a Life 116
35. The Exchange 120
36. How are the Mighty Fallen! 123
37. Stranger in Our Midst 127
38. My New Cousin 130

Table of Contents

39. War and Peace 133
40. Future Assured 135
41. Almost There 138
42. Hindsight is 20/20 140
43. That Moment 144
44. Leaving 147
45. Waterboarding 151
46. Coming to America 155
47. Nightmare #1 159
48. What is a Hero? 161
49. My Mother's House 164
Epilogue 167

Chapter 1

My Name Was Alec

My name is Allen. It's not the only name I've had, but it is the name I call myself today. Alec was the name I was born with on August, 17, 1941. It was on a cattle train. My mother and many others were fleeing Ukraine due to the invasion of the German army. I was born without a home, in a country that didn't want me, at the height of World War II, to a family without a compass. That was how I got my start.

My earliest memories were of the Displaced Persons Camps, where I spent my first years of life. When I close my eyes I still see the hollow faces of survivors of Auschwitz, Dachau and Treblinka. Live bodies carrying dead souls.

This, I was told, was how the world treated Jews: unwanted, unwelcome and exterminated when possible. "We need a home — The Holy Land," my grandfather would say. This was where my family would finally find a home. "The Holy Land is ours, Alec, as promised by God for more than 5,000 years." I can't say I knew exactly what he meant, but even at 5 years old, I knew that if God promised us Palestine, it was worth going.

Alec Yacobovich, age 2.

Chapter 2

Behind Barbed Wire...Again

In those early days after the war, my father and uncles formed a group to hunt the Nazis in Eastern Europe. I don't know where they got the guns, but often they left after dinner, not to return until sunrise. Some of my friends found out where they used to meet and hid in the bushes listening to them talk. That's how we learned what they were doing. I recall how fighting back made them men in the eyes of our family and the rest of our community.

During our time in the Displaced Persons Camp, a group of young men and women were sent from Palestine by the Haganah. In Hebrew, Haganah means "protectors." It was the Jewish Paramilitary Force in Palestine that would eventually become the Israel Defense Forces (IDF). These young men and women were sent to prepare us for a life in our own country.

They helped us to be kids again by taking us on field trips, playing soccer and other sports, or just doing physical activities like running, jumping and wrestling. They taught us Jewish history and, most importantly, they taught us to speak Hebrew. This language had not been spoken in over three thousand years, with the exception of during religious ceremonies. It had approximately 7,000 words in its entirety. Instead of being a dying language of the past, Hebrew is now spoken by over 10 million people, with over 35,000 words. Surely this was one of the greatest accomplishments of 20th century Jews who arose from the ashes of the Holocaust.

While the children played and learned, adults and the Haganah made plans to get us to Palestine. One night, we were awakened, bundled in warm clothing, hurried into big trucks and driven all night to a pier in Italy. We boarded two old steamships to sail east across the Mediterranean. "We are going to the Holy Land," my grandfather told me. I couldn't have been more excited.

We were at sea for eight days. The Haganah had three rifles and were teaching the adults how to shoot. The children continued to practice speaking Hebrew. Almost everyone got seasick during a storm. But one morning my grandfather woke me very early and hustled me onto the deck. He pointed east and said, "The Holy Land, Alec!" It was such an amazing sight it made me scream, "Palestine!" "No," said my grandfather, "That is Judea. Palestine is a name made up by people who hated us." Even in my excitement, I managed to hear every word he said.

Everyone was on deck dancing and singing. My grandfather had a Torah scroll that he carried with him throughout these tumultuous years. He held it out, giving everyone the opportunity to touch and kiss it, as is the custom.

Suddenly everything stopped. Out of the fog two British warships appeared. A sailor with a bullhorn ordered us to stop. British soldiers boarded our ship with guns and took control. We were being forced to sail to Cyprus. We were offloaded and taken to a camp with tents surrounded by barbed wire. We were in shock. Most of our people had survived Concentration Camps, then Displaced Persons Camps, and now we were behind barbed wire again. Men were cursing, some were praying, but most of the women were crying. The letdown was devastating. In sight of our promised land, yet behind barbed wire...again.

My Name Was Alec. A Memoir by Allen Jacoby

Isaac "Pop" Jacobovich (middle) in Displaced Persons Camp, Germany

Alec Jacobovich (left), Shaya Jacobovich (middle) in Displaced Persons Camp, Germany

Chapter 3

Finally Home

Life on Cyprus was different than the camps in Germany. Here we were guarded by British soldiers and could not leave.

The adults were restless. My father, "Pop," was a good athlete – especially boxing and soccer, so he convinced one of the truck drivers that delivered food to bring a soccer ball and boxing gloves. Soon the men were playing soccer and boxing. The women, when not busy cooking and washing, were on the sidelines cheering the men on.

The kids were busy too, since the Haganah managed to sneak some young men and women into the camp to continue our studies. In the morning we played sports, the afternoons were spent studying Hebrew, math, Bible stories and history. I loved the Bible stories because they weren't taught religiously, but as the history of our people from the time Abraham and his tribe migrated from Mesopotamia (now Iraq) to Canaan (now Israel), to the conquering of Israel by the Romans in 70 CE.

The Romans burned our temple in Jerusalem, exiled most of our people and, out of spite, renamed our country "Palaestina," after the Philistines. They were a warrior people from the Greek Islands, and our worst enemies during Biblical times. I already knew a lot of these stories, thanks to my grandfather.

Our history studies, were about the life of the Jews in the Diaspora after their expulsion from Israel, and their dream of returning to Zion (another name for Israel). I was only six years old and didn't comprehend everything, but it left a lifelong impression.

For the first three months on Cyprus, I was very busy. By that time, I already had a two-year-old brother who I took care of when the adults were busy. During this time, the Haganah made arrangements with the truck drivers to sneak us out of the camp to waiting boats that would take us to Palestine. Since Pop and my uncles were young men, they would be needed for the coming war with the Arab armies. My family was on the first boat. Unfortunately and sadly, it was night when we landed by mistake in Lebanon and had to walk across the border. Luckily we were not discovered and got to the northern city of Haifa. I was six years old. Finally, I was home.

Chapter 4

A Part of Something

We were home. Haifa. Miraculously, our entire family had survived: my grandparents, my parents, three uncles and their wives, two aunts and their husbands. There were kids, too. My brother Shaya and I were joined by three girl cousins. In total, there were fourteen adults and five children. Amazingly, we found a U-shaped 2-story house divided into seven apartments, accommodating all of our seven families.

It was February, 1947 and the end of the British Mandate was near, but their soldiers still patrolled the streets. We Jews still had small resistance groups fighting them and organizing for the coming war with the Arabs. Here were Jews fighting for a home. Here were Jews with pride.

The children started school as the Haganah tried to prepare for war, while the British tried to stop them. We kids were solicited to carry messages and bullets hidden in our schoolbags. At the age of 6, I was already helping my people earn their independence.

Meanwhile in school, I was learning about our people's history and was introduced to my heroes, King David and Judah Maccabee. These were Jews who forged our people's identity as a warrior nation thousands of years ago. There were modern fighters as well, such as Joseph Trumpeldor, a one-armed Russian soldier who immigrated to Palestine and gave his life defending early settlers. Yigal Yadin, Moshe Dayan and David Ben-Gurion were living, breathing heroes leading the fight for a Jewish homeland during the same time I was learning their names.

My heroes are my people! I wanted to be like all of them. I considered myself lucky to be Jewish and will never forget the excitement, joy and pride I felt when we won our statehood on May 14, 1948.

In Israel, I was a part of something, but I was also a kid in school with other kids

All surviving members of the family who emigrated to Israel celebrating my grandparents' wedding anniversary. Alec standing in back row (tallest)

Chapter 5

A New Name

---◆◇◆---

Before the British left, school was pretty normal. I was in first grade with three other boys and twenty girls. A boy's dream. We had a young teacher, Ruth, and all of us boys were so in love with her that we couldn't wait to get to school.

She used to call me "Dreamer" because my seat was next to the window and I would look out and daydream about being a warrior, like King David. I even had a slingshot and practiced with it every chance I got.

I loved school; it had become the center of my universe. As always, my favorite subject was the history of Israel – both ancient and modern. The Jewish people I saw in Israel were proud people who held their heads up, and walked with confidence, unlike the Jews from the Camps, who appeared to be afraid most of the time.

Two of the kids in my class, Danon and Rivka, were neighbors. In school we became close friends. We used to hang out together during recess and after school. Rivka's family came from Poland, and Danon's from Yemen. Rivka's family customs were similar to mine, but Danon's were more Middle Eastern. In his house, I was introduced to hummus, pitas, lamb's meat and stories from his grandfather about Jewish life as a minority in a Muslim country. They didn't have a Holocaust like in Europe, but were terribly mistreated and abused, and were as grateful and happy to be in Israel as the rest of us Europeans.

After World War II, and after the British left, survivors from Europe kept coming to Israel by the boatload. Our class, like the rest of the school, used to go down to the port to greet the new immigrants. A lot of them were survivors of Nazi Death Camps. Some of them we identified as "Muselmann," which was a German slang term used to describe Concentration Camp inmates who were near death due to exhaustion, starvation, or hopelessness. They were distinguished by their bloated bellies, tiny bodies, big heads and empty eyes. We would dress in blue pants and white shirts, and give them oranges grown in Israel while singing Hebrew songs. Most of the men either did not, or could not respond, but some of the women patted our heads or kissed us on the cheek, perhaps remembering a better time from their past.

It was not unusual to have a new kid join us at school, and one day one showed up. I immediately got into a fight with him. By the second day, we became best friends. He joined our little group to become one of the "Four Musketeers." The new kid, Meir, would remain my best friend for the next 65 years.

During our school years, Rivka, Danon, Meir and I were inseparable. We played marbles, soccer and practiced with our slingshots during recess. On Saturdays, we would hike Mount Carmel, explore the caves and sometimes stay up all night building a fire and roasting potatoes and pigeons we shot with our slingshots. Rivka was a real tomboy and kept up with us boys, but her father did not allow her to go on the overnight excursions.

It was 1947, and the U.N. voted to partition Palestine between the Arabs and the Jews. The Jews accepted the partition, but the Arabs did not. As anticipated, five Arab countries attacked Israel. Again our lives changed dramatically. Most of the men over the age of 18 went into the army. The school remained open, but attendance was not always possible. The city was bombed a few times, and local Arab snipers were shooting at pedestrians from the minarets on top of the mosques. It was no longer safe to walk the streets. All of us were scared.

Now we had to be driven to school in vans with no windows. They backed up to the windows on the ground level of the school where coal for the furnace was delivered. We'd slide down the chute into the basement and walk up to our classes. During recess, we either stayed in the classroom or played marbles in the hallways. At the end of the day we used stepladders to climb up to the windows and into the vans. In the beginning we thought it was fun, but when the van got hit by stray bullets, it became serious and some children were kept home by their mothers.

When 1949 rolled around, the war was finally over, and Israel miraculously won. The country regrouped and the men who survived the war came home. Our family was lucky. Pop and all my uncles came home safely.

Now I finally had to deal with my own serious issue. In the Jewish tradition, a Jewish boy is not named until he is 8 days old. That's when he is circumcised and given a Hebrew name. Because I spent the first 2 months of my life on a cattle train, then in the Displaced Persons Camps, and then the war in Israel, I had not been circumcised. I was called Alec, which was a common name given to boys in Europe, but not a Hebrew name. In 1949, my time had come. I was scared, but there was no avoiding it. So it was done. To be honest, it was very painful, especially when urinating, but it was done and I was given my Hebrew name, "Yechiel," which means "God shall live." To this day I do not know who chose that name. I was not crazy about it and neither were my relatives.

Everyone continued to call me Alec, and some still do.

Graduating grammar school-Haifa. Yechiel (back row, far right), Danon (back row, next to Yechiel), Rivka (third row, 4th from right), Meir (front row, left), teacher Ruth (second row, center)

Chapter 6

A Word about Manhood

After the war had ended and my manhood had been (slightly) shortened, school and family returned to normal. My brother Ben was born, as were more cousins.

In school, the four of us became even closer and we boys were still in love with our teacher, Ruth. (Eight years later in 1956 during the war with Egypt known as the "Sinai Campaign," Ruth's jeep would run over a mine, killing her. It hit us all very hard. I could not stop crying at her funeral).

Our little group of friends began hiking on Mt. Carmel again, with slingshots to shoot down pigeons, and potatoes to cook with them over a fire. Life was good again.

On our way home one morning, we saw a house with a fenced-in yard, and in the yard were chickens. We decided then and there, that the next time we went up to our cave, instead of a puny pigeon, we would steal one of the chickens to cook. On a late

Friday night, we put our plan into action. Meir, Danon and I jumped over the fence, grabbed a chicken, killed it, and took it up to the cave, hiding it for later. On our way home, we saw two adults walking towards us. Meir whispered, "I don't like this," but it was too late. They grabbed us and took us to the police station. We were put in our own cell with concrete floors and a bucket in which we could relieve ourselves. We were terrified.

At daylight, the sergeant sent a policeman to get our parents. The mothers of Meir and Danon came in at noon. They talked to the sergeant, screamed at their children, and took them home. My father showed up later in the afternoon and talked with the sergeant. Then he came to my cell. He didn't scream. All he said was that he would come get me the next day, and left. It was the worst night of my young life, but I never took anything that didn't belong to me again. Lesson learned!

Chapter 7

My Secret Identity

After the "Chicken Affair," life returned to normal. The war was over, but I kept dreaming of one day becoming an officer in the paratroopers.

My mother, however, did not share my dreams. To her, money became more important than her family, or Israel. Dishonesty ran through our house like a corrosive thread. Secrets and lies were commonplace. My mother belittled my father all the time, and had affairs behind his back. Pop got drunk and took his anger out on us. In order to make more money, my mother began soliciting prostitutes out of our home, where my two brothers and I were being raised. When she got caught, Pop took the blame and went to jail. While he was imprisoned, my mother had an affair with a boarder, which led to the birth of my third brother, Ezra.

It was 1953. I was 12 years old and the shame that burned in my stomach was too much to bear. The more I saw, the more I felt different from my family. By the time I was 13 – the age when boys tread on the cusp between the innocence of childhood and the responsibility of adulthood – my naïve dreams gasped their last breath

One day, I was looking at photos in an old album and came across one with three young men. The one on the left got all my attention. I felt a physical connection to him. I kept the picture and looked at it every chance I had. The following Friday, my cousin Molly and I went to our grandparents' home for Shabbat dinner as usual. I took the photo out and asked them who the man was. They got visibly upset and started talking to each other in Russian. The only word I understood was, "Misha."

The next day, I went to see my Uncle Zalman. He told me the truth: Pop was not my biological father. My mother and Misha were married in 1940 and lived in a small village in the Ukraine. Misha was studying for his law degree when World War II broke out. He was drafted into the army. In 1941, when the Germans invaded the Ukraine, Misha was killed. My mother and most of the villagers got on a train headed for the capital, Kiev, to escape the advancing Germans. The trip took two months and I was born on the way.

This information spun my identity off its axis. I wondered if my biological father was the man of honor I wanted to be. As things got worse at home, I decided I couldn't stay in that house any longer. I had to get out.

The Picture: My biological father, Misha (far left)

Chapter 8

Belonging

On my 14th birthday, I packed a small backpack and ran away from my family. For the first two days, I slept on a bench at the train station. My 10-year-old brother, Shaya, was the only one who knew where I was. He brought me food each day and told me that the police were called and were looking for me. On the third day, I decided it was time to move on. Shaya stole some money from my parents to give to me. I told him that I would let my friends, Meir and Rivka, know where I was when I could and he should stay in touch with them. I kissed him goodbye, and went to the highway to hitchhike. I headed south for no particular reason.

Within ten minutes, I got a ride on a small truck. Five minutes later, the young truck driver figured out what I was doing. At first, I was afraid that he would take me to the police, but he was cool. He asked me if I had a plan, which of course I didn't. He said, "Let's get some breakfast and talk."

He told me he's a member of a kibbutz called Neve Eitan. The Jewish Agency sponsored kids like me who, for differing reasons, don't live with their families or have a family. They set these kids up in various kibbutzim. They will go to school and work, the same as the rest of the kibbutz members. Of course, it's not a place to hide, and the Agency would notify my parents. It took me about ten seconds to decide. I knew Pop would let me do it. Two hours later, I was in the barracks-style dormitory, being introduced to twenty other kids approximately my age.

A few words about a kibbutz. It's a small collective settlement, mostly with an agricultural purpose. Neve Eitan had approximately 300 families. It was basically a socialist way of life. Every family had a small 2 bedroom house, with all the same features. We all ate together in a large dining room and everyone had a job in the kibbutz. The adults worked the whole day. The kids, who lived in dormitories, went to school in the kibbutz, then worked four hours a day. We had 425 milk cows, 2 bulls, 24 fish ponds, chicken coops, cotton fields, and orange groves. We all had steady jobs.

I worked with the cows. I milked them, took them out to pasture, and helped deliver their newborn. Some jobs, like washing dishes in the kitchen, were rotated. When it was time to take fish out of the ponds and take them to market, we all pitched in. We had our own trucks to take the goods to market and also bartered with other kibbutzim. For example, the kibbutz next door to ours let us use their combine to pick our cotton, and we loaned them our bulls to inseminate their cows.

Life for me on the kibbutz was great. I finally had a sense of belonging. My ultimate goal was to be an officer in the IDF. I had already decided to enlist at age 17.

Yechiel at Kibbutz Neve Eitan (4th from front)

Yechiel at Kibbutz Neve Eitan (far left)

Chapter 9

Heroes

I loved my three years in the kibbutz. I went to school, I swam and I worked. I grew strong, in a life of my own choosing.

One day, I finished early and went to the pool for a swim. I saw a boy in the pool doing laps, with an adult using a stopwatch to time him. I jumped in and started swimming in the lane next to him. When I got out, the man with the stopwatch came over and asked, "Where did you learn to swim?" I answered, "I'm from Haifa and there is a big ocean there." He smiled, we shook hands, and he told me his name was Avner. He was coaching his brother, Uzi, for a swim tournament and asked if I wanted to join the Hapoal swim team. (In Israel we had two main sports organizations: Hapoal and Maccabees). I agreed right away, thus launching my competitive swimming career. I loved swimming, but school and work continued to occupy most of my time.

Without proper time or training, we were not exactly world class swimmers, but I loved competing, so we did the best we could.

My favorite race was the 100 meter freestyle. No one in Israel had managed to swim it under one minute. At one meet, I felt sick so Avner told me not to worry about pacing myself – just go all out. I did just that, and when I finished I saw all the timekeepers standing at my lane. I looked at Avner, he said that "[I] did the first 50 meters in 28 seconds, so all the timers came to my lane thinking I was going to break the one minute mark." Ultimately, my time that meet was 1.008. Close, but no cigar.

At the kibbutz, I looked up to the members who came of age and already served in the army. They usually served in the paratroopers. Some fought in the War of Independence and were still fighting the ongoing war with Arab terrorists. Some of them were even storied heroes. The most famous was my boss at the dairy, Shimon, or as he was (and still is) known all over Israel, "Katcha." I loved the Friday nights when his friends came to visit. They would build a fire and sit around, telling war stories. Sometimes the commander of the paratroopers, Arik Sharon, would come. He would eventually become the Prime Minister of Israel.

On one such night, I told Sharon that I planned to enlist on my 17th birthday, and that I wanted to become a paratrooper. He smiled and said, "I will keep an eye out for you."

Yechiel (far right) at Israeli swim meet.

Yechiel (top) swimming competitively.

Chapter 10

Get Out Jew!

Though military service in Israel is mandatory, I saw it as an honor; a chance to live up to the noble characters of my heroes of old and from the generation that came before me. I wish I could say that building a brighter future for Israel was the only thing that drove me, but it wasn't. Here's the story of what lit my fire:

Usually when I didn't swim on Saturday, I would take the cows out to pasture, riding on one of our horses. One particular Saturday, the horse was needed back at the kibbutz, so one of my friends rode out with me. When we got to the field, he rode the horse back to where it was needed. I sat down under a tree reading a book. As soon as my friend left, I was jumped by three Arabs and beaten to within an inch of my life. With every rib they broke, and tooth they kicked loose, they kept cursing and screaming for Jews to get out of Palestine.

I felt the hatred and threat we Israelis faced. They began to cut my throat. I looked up in time to see them shot dead by army sharpshooters. My friend had ridden back and, when he saw the attack, rushed to get help. If not for the IDF, I would not have survived. My idealism was now mixed with firsthand knowledge of what Israel was up against. A surrounding enemy that would do anything to destroy us. I wanted to join the army now, more than ever.

I was in bad shape with broken ribs, a broken nose and internal bleeding. It took three months to recover. The first week I was in a lot of pain, and when the bones started healing, I still had to deal with internal bleeding and difficulty breathing. Consequently, I spent most of my time reading and reliving the past. I especially thought about my relationship with Pop and what a special man he was.

Yechiel, after being attacked by Arabs.

Chapter 11

Pop

My father, or "Pop," as everyone called him, was a gentle giant. My first memories of him were when my brother Shaya was born. I was 4 years old. We lived in a small village somewhere in Russia. My mother and Pop were sewing what looked like heavy military coats, while I was playing and watching my baby brother.

One night we were bundled up in the heavy coats and our entire family, including uncles, aunts and grandparents, walked the whole night across the border to the area of Germany that was controlled by the USA. Most of the night, Pop carried me on his shoulders. He had me repeat the word, "kukuruza," which meant 'corn' in Russian, because I couldn't pronounce my "r's" (I still can't).

When I got older, my grandfather told me that after the war, Pop and a friend of his were smuggling Jews out of Russia to the Displaced Persons Camp in Germany. Holocaust survivors didn't want to live under communist rule. Pop had been doing this for a few months and on the last trip, he took our entire family to the Displaced Persons Camp from which we would eventually depart for Palestine.

Everyone loved Pop. In the Displaced Persons Camp, he organized soccer games for the adults and kids; he built a boxing ring to teach the kids how to box; and he arranged, with the American MP's who were guarding the camp, to bring him chocolate and cigarettes to distribute. He even managed to find me a tricycle.

Everyone loved Pop, except my mother, who was always on his case, berating him for not "wheeling and dealing" like some of the other men. It just wasn't in his nature. He was always a "straight shooter." Even when he punished me, it was always for a reason, like when he left me overnight at the police station for stealing the chicken. He understood when I ran away from home and when I volunteered to be a paratrooper and went to the officer's academy.

On my first weekend pass after getting my paratrooper wings, I went to see him. He took me to the Haifa docks where he worked to show me off and told everyone there, "My son, the paratrooper, is going to be an officer." Then he took me to a bar where he bought drinks for everyone and I had my first vodka with him.

Pop was not educated or sophisticated, but he was one of the best human beings I ever knew. He made me realize that blood does not make family. I was proud to be his son and I know my youngest brother feels the same.

Pop holding young Alec.

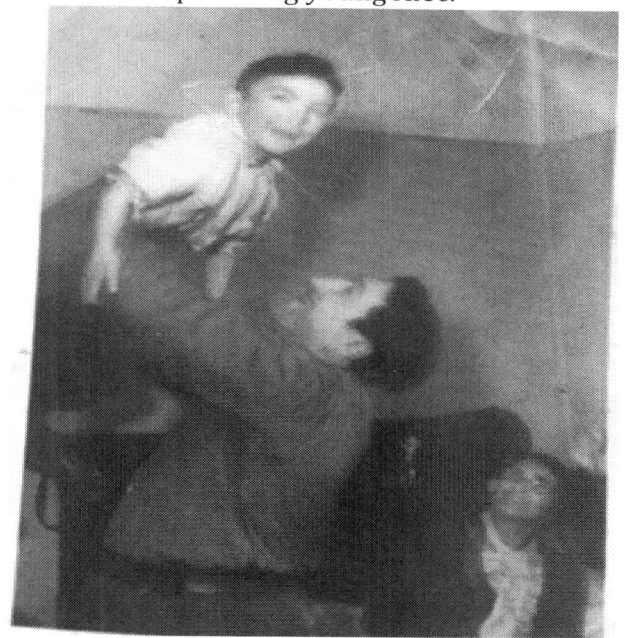

Yechiel and Pop at the northern border of Israel and Lebanon.

Chapter 12

I'm in the Army Now

August 17, 1958, I was at the enlistment base in a small town called Atlit. The great irony of this place being the enlistment base for the IDF, is its history. Atlit was home to a detention camp built by the British in the 1930's. It housed Jewish refugees fleeing from Europe and nearby Muslim countries. There were wooden barracks surrounded by fences of barbed wire and watchtowers. Upon arrival, refugees were deloused, told to undress, and led to showers. Men and women were separated by barbed wire. Sound familiar? Tens-of-thousands of Jewish refugees were interned at this camp during the 1930's and 1940's. Even some of the passengers captured from the famous ship "Exodus" were interned here.

On that day – my 17th birthday – I clutched papers signed by Pop, giving me permission to enlist early. Within two hours, I was checked by a doctor, had my hair cut, and wound up in a green uniform standing at attention with another hundred guys, just like me, being yelled at by a sergeant. We were issued a kitbag, canteen, rifle (no bullets), and assigned a bed in the barracks.

We didn't walk. Everything was done running. We were given numbers. No staff member used our names. For the next three months, we were broken down both physically and mentally, so they could retrain us as soldiers.

After the first week, we were issued ammunition, bayonets, and hand grenades, and we learned to use them. We were punished for every infraction.

I remember one Friday afternoon, the entire camp was standing at attention while the camp commander was talking to us. Somebody in my platoon farted. After the commander finished his speech, the sergeant ordered us into groups of two. He told us to grab empty fifty-gallon drums with which we had to capture the fart. We spent four hours running all over the grounds until he mercifully agreed we had completed the task.

Another day one of the guys tripped on a loose bootlace. The entire company in full gear and at attention stood in the middle of the parade grounds with the sun beating down on us while our sergeant spent over two hours explaining to us how to properly tie our boots.

All good things must come to an end. In mid-November, I was told to go to the commander's office with three other guys. We stood at attention thinking, "What now?" He smiled and said, "You four are done here. Pack your stuff, turn in your rifles and be by the front gate in thirty minutes for the truck that will take you to Tel Nof. You are going to be paratroopers." We started smiling and he said, "Go ahead, smile. By tomorrow this place will feel like a walk in the park."

The four of us became close friends for the next few years. We were Yakov ("Yaki"), Zvi ("Zveeka"), Aria ("Ari') and me ("Yechi"). We were together on some great missions, and one very terrible mission that would haunt me for the rest of my life.

Yechiel training in boot camp.

Boot camp training

Yechiel (far left) training at boot camp.

Yechiel (left) balancing at boot camp.

Yechiel (6th from right) being transported to Tel Nof to become a paratrooper.

Chapter 13

Becoming a Paratrooper

We arrived at Tel Nof on Sunday afternoon, unloaded our gear in the barracks and went to the parade ground to meet the officers and camp commander. He told us that before getting our wings, we would have to undergo three months of training and complete six jumps from 1200 feet, including a night jump and a jump over the ocean. He said we would be treated like soldiers, and expected 60% of us would finish the training and become paratroopers.

After meeting our sergeants and officers, we had dinner in the mess hall, then returned to the barracks to unpack. Afterwards, we went to the armory for weapons and other supplies. By 9:00 P.M., we were in bed. This was by far the easiest day we'd had since enlisting.

For the first 2-1/2 months we went through the hardest physical training. We did hundreds of push-ups and chin-ups a day. We practiced shooting from different positions. We climbed mountains and crawled through swamps. We ran and ran and ran – 10 km in the morning and another 5 km at night (sometimes more). By this time, 40% washed out just like the commander had predicted. I made it, and so did my three friends.

The last 2 weeks were spent learning how to parachute. My most exciting jump was the night jump. The plane was an old Dakota with room for 24 jumpers. We stood up in two rows, hooked up the static line onto the cables overhead, and checked the chute of the guy in front of us. The jump masters opened the door. The noise was overwhelming. That night I was first in line. I moved to the door and waited for the red light to turn green. When it did, I was out the door. The retreating rumble of the engines was all that remained after the momentary explosion of noise upon exiting. There wasn't a lot of room inside the plane, so jumping into the darkness was liberating. Outside it was quiet, with a lot of space and fresh air. Suddenly, I felt the tug as the parachute canopy erupted, unfurling above. It felt euphoric.

When we got back to camp, the sergeant told us that we would be climbing Masada tomorrow, where we will get our wings.

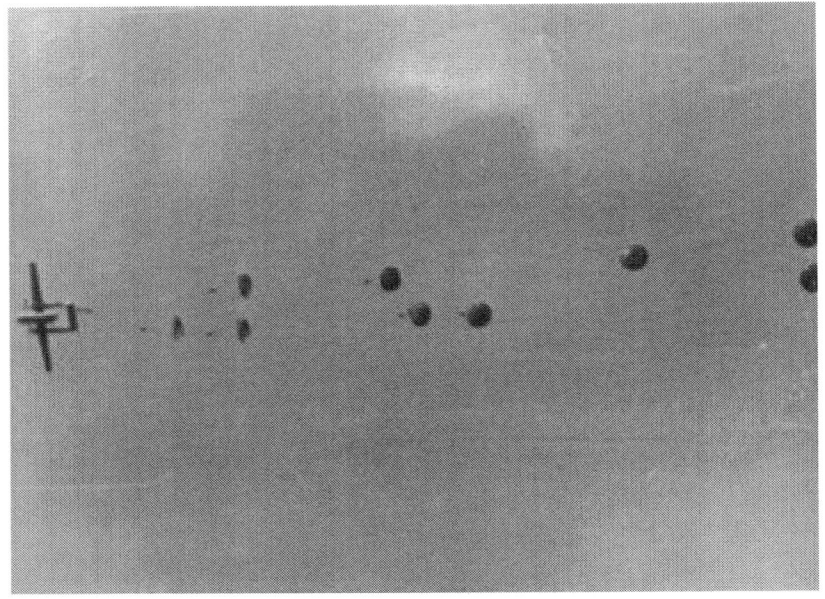

Training jump with entire company.

Yechiel parachuting with stretcher for wounded.

Yechiel parachuting into water.

Entire company parachuting into water.

Chapter 14

Getting My Wings

Masada is basically an enormous rock near the Dead Sea, in the middle of nowhere. The Dead Sea is the lowest spot on earth. The mountain is very steep, rising approximately 460 feet on the east and 300 feet on the west. On top is a plateau measuring about 1800 ft. x 900 ft. In those days, the only way to reach the top was by the "snake," a very narrow dirt road. On top is the remnant of a palace built by King Herod of Israel sometime in the beginning of the Roman era. It was very hard to get to the top (now there is a tram you can ride).

In 70 CE, when the Romans put down the Jewish revolt in Israel and burned the temple in Jerusalem, some of the remaining Jewish fighters and their families escaped and took over Masada. They numbered approximately 920 men, women and children. The Romans laid siege but couldn't get their equipment to the top, so they used slave labor to build a dirt ramp. Once they got to the top, the Jews realized that the fight would be over in a matter of days. They had a meeting and decided to commit suicide so as not to become slaves. Every head of family was to kill his wife and children. The last man was to fall on his own sword. When the Romans breached the walls, they found two women and four children who had somehow survived. Since that time, Masada has been a symbol of freedom to the Jewish people.

The day after our last parachute jump, we rode trucks to Masada and climbed to the top. There was Ariel Sharon, our commander, standing by a small table with 28 paratrooper wings lined up. As each of us went by, he personally affixed our wings over our heart. I can't remember the exact words he used, but his message was clear. He welcomed us as the new warriors of the 202 Paratrooper Brigade. He said that our mission was to make sure that the Jewish people do not ever have to choose between freedom and suicide again. To that end, we will fight and keep on fighting and never give up – not ever – and before we die we must look back and be able to say that we never gave up. It's not enough to fight and never give up. We have to win -- win or die.

Then his aide brought out vodka and paper cups. We all had a drink. The last thing I heard him say was, "Welcome to my family."

Chapter 15

A Job Well Done

When we came back from Masada, we got a weekend pass. After getting a ride to Haifa, I went to my old school and waited for my friends, Meir and Rivka, to come out. During the past three years, they had visited me in Neve Eitan a few times, but once I enlisted early, not so much. Now, they too were getting ready to join the military, like every other 18 year-old.

That weekend I stayed at Meir's house and visited with my family. I was a big hit in my dress uniform, with red boots, red beret and wings on my chest. It was a great weekend. On Sunday morning, Rivka's father drove me back to camp.

The next three months were busy. Our brigade had four battalions and every battalion had three companies of sixty each. Every company had three platoons of twenty each, plus support personnel. My three friends and I were together in one platoon, with no time to socialize. When we were in camp, we trained like before, often parachuting in the desert near the Dead Sea for maneuvers with other branches of the IDF (Israel Defense Forces).

We also had real missions. On one such mission, our Sergeant, three others from my platoon, and I set up an ambush near the Jordan River. We had intelligence that Fedayeens (Arab terrorists) were infiltrating from Jordan. Sometimes they would come over to steal livestock, and other times they came to kill.

This was my third such mission. At about 2:00 AM, we saw three infiltrators cross the river. They stopped about 20 feet from us to have a smoke. We looked to our Sergeant who hand signaled us to move quietly as close as we could. They were so surprised when we stood up next to them, our weapons pointed at their heads. They dropped their rifles and raised their hands in surrender. No shooting. No injuries.

We took them back to camp and handed them over to M-I (Military Intelligence). Everyone was excited. At Friday night dinner, Commander Sharon cited us on a job well done.

The next day, I was asked to join the Recon (Reconnaissance) Unit. The Recon Unit is a small 'special ops' unit with only 27 men – mostly Officers, Sergeants and Corporals (no Privates). Their training was more specialized, making it the unit that was assigned the most difficult operations. I was made a Corporal the day I joined.

Unfortunately, I was only a part of this unit for two weeks. At the end of the second week, the Master Sergeant read out names of soldiers heading to Sergeant's school. My friends Yaki, Zveeka and Ari were on the list. Then he named 14 men to be sent to Officer's Academy. My name was on that list.

I was 18 years old and on my way to being an officer in the best unit, of the best brigade, in the best army in the world. I would be one of the warriors charged with defending the Jewish people in our ancient homeland.

I was proud.

Yechiel's (center, holding a mortar) first command of paratrooper platoon.

Yechiel (center, back row) with his platoon. Ari (back row, sunglasses. Zveeka (front row, left). Yaki (back row, 2nd from right).

Chapter 16

The Academy

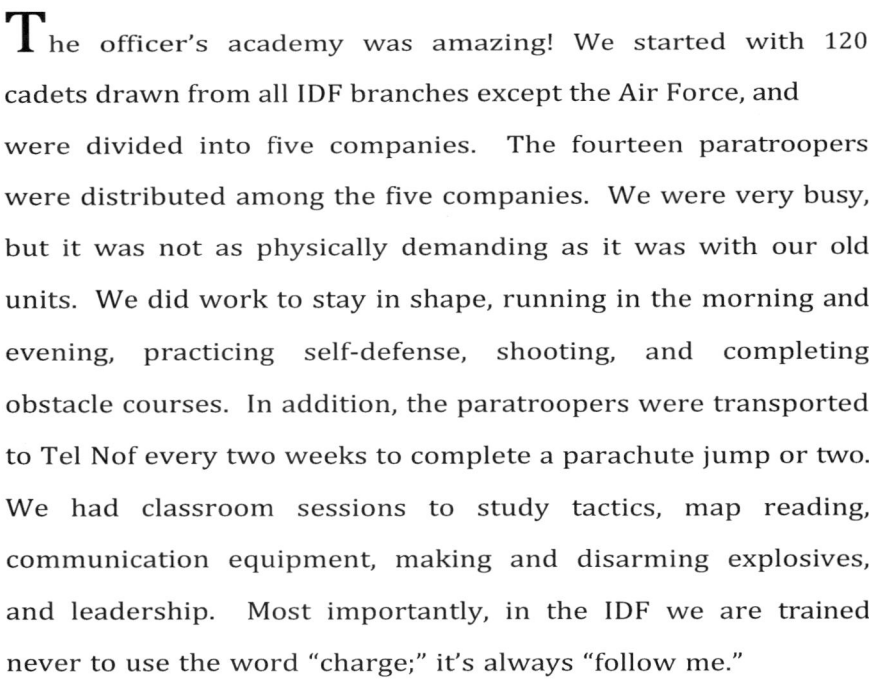

The officer's academy was amazing! We started with 120 cadets drawn from all IDF branches except the Air Force, and were divided into five companies. The fourteen paratroopers were distributed among the five companies. We were very busy, but it was not as physically demanding as it was with our old units. We did work to stay in shape, running in the morning and evening, practicing self-defense, shooting, and completing obstacle courses. In addition, the paratroopers were transported to Tel Nof every two weeks to complete a parachute jump or two. We had classroom sessions to study tactics, map reading, communication equipment, making and disarming explosives, and leadership. Most importantly, in the IDF we are trained never to use the word "charge;" it's always "follow me."

My favorite exercise was planning then executing a raid. When my turn came up in the third month, I was given command of a company and told that my mission was to raid a radar station on

Mt. Tabor. (There really is a Mt. Tabor in Central Israel with a radar station on top.)

I was given maps, radio equipment and trucks that would drop us 5 km from the target. After that, we were on our own. I divided my company into three platoons, picked two Cadets to command two of them; I commanded the third platoon, along with command for the overall mission. One of the instructors came along to monitor. Another company was placed on the mountain as enemy guards. The exercise began at noon. I took my company out of the base to brief and practice.

Mt. Tabor is relatively flat on top – about 3 km x 3 km. My instructors showed me plans indicating that the company guarding the radar station was on the north side of the plateau, and would have 18 men around the radar station, and 18 men about 2 km south of the station guarding the access road.

I decided we would all climb the mountain from the west slope. When we got close to the top, my first platoon went south and got into position to attack the men guarding the road. The second platoon set up halfway between the station and the access road. My platoon set up in position to attack the station.

We synchronized our watches. At 2:00 am, the first platoon attacked the access road (we used blanks). As soon as the shooting started, the units guarding the station rushed out to help the unit guarding the road, at which point they were ambushed by the second platoon With no one left at the station, we simply walked in. I kept two men with me to set the explosive, and sent the rest of my men to help the other two units. Thirty minutes after starting the attack, the monitor called the exercise. It was a complete success.

During the debriefing, the base commander wanted to know how I came up with the plan. I told him how I like Bible stories, and that I got the tactic from Joshua who used it to capture a Canaanite city called, "Ai."

He smiled and said that it would be part of our future training.

Chaim Laskov (Chief of Staff) visiting Academy. Yechiel (2nd from right) chosen to be part of welcoming honor guard

Yechiel marching at parade during Laskov's visit. (right column, 2nd Cadet).

Chapter 17

Graduation

April, 1960, I graduated and became an officer in the IDF 202 Paratrooper Brigade. The Recon Unit with an unmatched record.

I graduated at the top of my company. Out of the five companies, four of the top graduates were Paratroopers. No surprise there.

We returned to Tel Nof on a Sunday morning. I reported to the Captain, leader of the small recon unit, who informed me that I'd only be in the unit for one month, then would take over as second-in-command of Company B. I realized that the only reason I was with the recon unit for a month was to gain specialized training. Up until then I had about 30 jumps – all with a static line -- meaning I hook the line to the cable in the plane, jump out and the chute opens by itself. Now I have to learn freestyle jumping. We jump from higher altitudes (10,000 to 15,000 feet), free-fall, and pull a handle to open the chute. I couldn't wait to start.

Every jump was an adventure. Parachutes have a nasty habit of not letting you know they're not working until it's too late. Once you are out of the door of the plane, there's no way to get back in. Nevertheless, it was exciting. I am not sure I can talk about some of the specialized training we received, but I completed ten freestyle jumps and, for my final, had to make a night jump by myself from a small plane 15,000 feet in the air and land in a small clearing in a forest with a small building in the middle — all without being seen by the building's guards.

I took off at midnight with just the pilot of the two-seater. I was told the pilot would drop me at 15,000 feet about 2 km from the target. Besides the primary chute, I had a reserve, my Uzi, a compass, and altitude gauge. Thirty minutes after takeoff, the pilot signaled to get ready. I stood by the door as the pilot gave a "thumbs up." I was out the door, counted to 10, and pulled the handle. A jerk and a thud, and I was floating. The darkness below was impenetrable. In theory, I was descending toward the clearing, but when you are suspended in midair from a delicate piece of silk in the darkness, theory is just that —theory.

Slowly as I descended, the ground below me began to take shape by the light of the moon. I was slightly south of the clearing, dropping towards the woods. I adjusted my trajectory and descended into the grassy clearing as close to the trees as I could get without impaling myself.

As I landed and started gathering my chute, the jump instructor walked out of the woods and said, "Well done, Yechi. You are good to go."

Top five Cadets (one from each company). Yechiel (far right).

Graduation. Shaking hands with the Commander of the Academy.

Trophy for earning the Overall Top Cadet Award.

Chapter 18

Israel's Superheroes

Finally, I was done with training and got my assignment. I was second-in-command of a paratrooper recon company. The unit was considered to be one of the most experienced and efficient special forces units in the world. It set standards of excellence in tactics, strategy, training, and endurance that have been emulated by virtually every elite military group in the world. The unit bred wolves and turned expert soldiers into lean, effective hunters and killers of terrorists, which is what I became.

We were also the superheroes of Israel – unmistakable in our red boots and berets. Children didn't want to be Mickey Mantle or John Wayne when they grew up; they wanted to be us. After all, baseball was only a game and movies were make-believe. We were the real McCoy. We were heroes because we stood between Israel and the Arab Fedayeen.

In the late 1950's and early 1960's, loose bands of "Palestinians" had begun to organize and attack wherever and however they could, creating fear and causing as much harm as possible. They were the precursors of what the world knows today as Hezbollah, Hamas, Al Qaeda and Isis. They were zealots, and fanatically willing to die for their cause.

Death wish or not, the Fedayeen knew us and were scared of us, because we crossed into Gaza and Jordan when we learned that they were planning to bomb our buses or raid our settlements. They were scared because, even when they did manage an attack, we'd be the ones on their asses as they were running away.

When we weren't fighting Fedayeens, we scouted and patrolled, searched, observed and reported, hunted, captured and evaded. From some missions, we came home smiling; others left us in tears when we lost friends.

This was my life after the academy. My mission, as I saw it, was to defend my people. I believed then, and still do now, what Golda Meir said: "If the Arabs put down their weapons, there would be peace in the Middle East tomorrow. If the Jews put down their weapons, there would be no Israel."

Chapter 19

The Tent

After my assignment as second-in-command of the recon company, I met with my commanding officer, Capt. "Dudu," who told me there was going to be a new company. He was given command of this new company, and asked that I be part of the command structure.

The company consisted of 27 experienced paratroopers who formed three platoons of nine men each. He asked that I recruit three sergeants, one for each platoon. I immediately asked for Yaki and Zveeka, which he approved. I told him they will find and get a third sergeant.

I then asked the Captain for permission to erect a tent away from the barracks. Of course, he wanted to know why, so I told him: When Moses led the Hebrews out of Egypt, they had to fight their way to Canaan. Most of the fighting was up close and personal with knives, spears and clubs. Very bloody. Moses ordered tents be erected at the edge of the camp as a refuge for fighters who were affected by the killing. He knew that they needed time away from everyone to process their feelings, meditate, and somehow come to terms with the killing.

It's never easy for a normal human to kill – not even when it's justified – especially when it's close up. I believed that staying away from the rest of the camp and normal routine would help. Dudu looked at me and said, "I don't see a kippah (traditional skullcap) on your head. Are you religious?" "No," I said, "but I like reading the Bible as a history book, a history of our people." He thought for a minute and said, "Go ahead, Yechi. It makes sense."

Little did I know at that moment that, within a week, we would have the first soldier use the tent. It would be me.

Returning from patrolling the border.

Chapter 20

Mission for Rivka

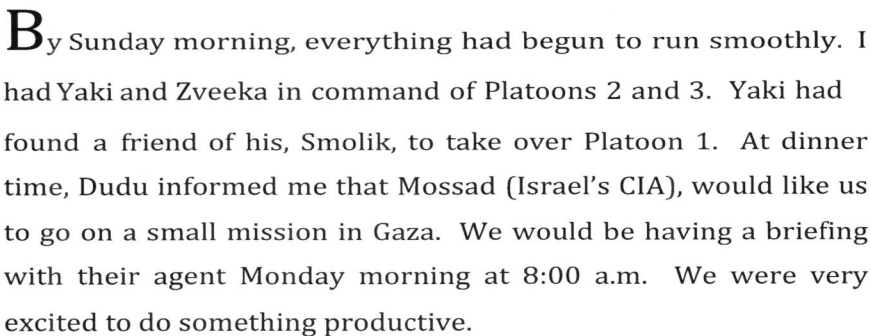

By Sunday morning, everything had begun to run smoothly. I had Yaki and Zveeka in command of Platoons 2 and 3. Yaki had found a friend of his, Smolik, to take over Platoon 1. At dinner time, Dudu informed me that Mossad (Israel's CIA), would like us to go on a small mission in Gaza. We would be having a briefing with their agent Monday morning at 8:00 a.m. We were very excited to do something productive.

At 8:00 a.m., I walked into the captain's office. The Mossad agent was already there. The agent stood and said, "Hi, Yechi." I stood there with my mouth open in shock. Finally I said, "Shalom, Rivka." It was my school friend from Haifa. Dudu couldn't stop laughing. Finally Rivka got down to business.

The Mossad was tracking a leader of a small Fedayeen gang. He controlled about a dozen to two dozen terrorists, and usually traveled with three bodyguards. They would cross the border from Gaza to steal livestock and cause damage to homes and equipment.

Two weeks before, they had injured two and killed one Israeli, so the decision was made to capture him alive. They had reliable information that he spent his nights in a small village with his bodyguards about 2 km from the border. We reviewed maps and pictures and it was decided that Smolik, Yaki and I would go in that night to take a look.

We got into Gaza at 2:00 a.m. on Tuesday and found the house. Watching from a distance of about 200 yards, we saw two guards sitting in chairs – one in front of the house by the door, and one in the back. They were mostly sleeping, and when they were awake, they were smoking. At 6:00 a.m., we saw two men come out of the house – one was our guy.

The next night, I came back to Gaza with Yaki and watched the same routine as the night before. When we got back to our camp, we got together with Smolik, Capt. Dudu and a corporal named David. I explained what we saw and said that I only wanted four of us to do the mission: Yaki, Smolik, David and myself. Smolik and I would take out the guards and stay outside the house for cover. Yaki and David would grab the target. Dudu let Rivka know and asked her to be at our camp Saturday morning with help to take the prisoner.

We got a Command Car and a driver and left our camp at 10:00pm on Friday. The driver dropped us off 1 km from the border where he would wait for us. We got to the village at 2:00 a.m., where Smolik and I took off to quietly take out the guards.

Contrary to what you see in movies, you cannot take a guard out silently with a firearm. There is no such thing as a silencer – only noise suppressors. They will suppress the noise escaping from the gun barrel, but not from the breech, so there is still noise. For complete silence, you use a knife. Smolik and I had extensive training in hand-to-hand combat, especially with knives. We sneaked up on the guards and took them out. Afterwards, Yaki and David entered through the front door. The bodyguard jumped up with a gun and David shot him. Our target stood with his hands in the air, and we hustled him to our Command Car. By 6:00 a.m., we had turned him over to Rivka and two MP's.

It was a successful mission, but when the adrenaline rush was over, I looked at my guys and said, "I'm going to the recovery tent." Smolik, who just threw up, said, "Me, too." We looked at David and he nodded, "Me, too."

Chapter 21

The Defenders

The three of us spent two days in the Recovery Tent. Yaki brought food and drinks. The Captain and camp doctor came by to see how we were doing. Mostly, we just talked with each other.

Smolik was a Sabra (born in Israel). David was from Poland and came to Israel with his parents. His grandparents died in a concentration camp. The Nazis murdered over six million Jews – 2-1/2 million of them children. Just about every Jewish person lost family members in concentration camps.

I asked David and Smolik if they had killed before. David said he hadn't, but Smolik told us that in his old unit, he was part of a 5-man team that set up an ambush near the Jordan River. They got into a gunfight with three terrorists and killed them. Since everyone was shooting, it wasn't as personal as what we did. All the same, he got sick and threw up.

"How about you?" Smolik asked me. I told them I never killed anyone before, but when I was attacked by the three Fedayeen, they were shot in front of me. Even though I was semi-conscious, I too got sick. Then, David and Smolik wanted to know how the tent came to be. I explained to them the story from the Bible, and how even our ancient warriors were affected by killing and needed a place to mentally recover.

I told them that before the mission, I was in a different mental zone, but when it was over, I couldn't stop thinking about the men we killed and how hard their deaths will affect their families. I told them I needed this tent to sort out the reasons why I wanted to be a soldier. It wasn't because I liked to kill; it was because I wanted to protect my people.

We were not killers. We were members of the Israel *Defense* Forces. We were defenders. The tent helped me remember that, and to cope with the contradictory feelings that are brought up when we must take a life. After a while, Smolik said, "I think every army should have a tent." I said, "Not every army is a defensive force. Our enemies are trying to kill us. They will never have a tent. We kill in self-defense to protect our nation. We value and respect life. We will always need a tent."

After a while they fell asleep. I went outside for a smoke and thought about how I believed in Israel. Our reborn country was still young and rough around the edges, but there was a magical optimism in the air mixed with patriotism and love of country, so strong and precious. I had never known anything like it before or after. I went back into the tent, looked at my two brothers, and went to sleep.

My sleep was troubled. Tormented, even. I kept waking with the smell of blood that turned my stomach, the acrid smoke that burned my eyes. It was painfully clear. I realized that decisions made, and actions taken, are impossible to reverse. These thoughts and senses continued to torment me when I tried to sleep. After all these years, they still do.

Yechiel, Smolik and David (left to right) in The Tent.

Chapter 22

Rewards

We left the tent on a Thursday afternoon. Yaki was taking the company out for a 5 km run, so we joined in. It felt good to be back with my guys. At dinnertime, Sharon told us that the next day he wanted everyone clean shaven and in a clean uniform. He ordered us to be in the mess hall promptly at 1800 hours because we would be having a surprise guest for Shabbat dinner.

The next evening, the first thing I noticed walking into the mess hall was a small platform left of the kitchen door, a microphone, and a piano. Next to the piano was a small table with two Shabbat candles. Once we were all seated, the kitchen door opened and a guy came in and sat on the piano bench. Then out walked Shoshana Damari. She was the most popular singer in Israel at the time, especially committed to the IDF, entertaining troops whenever she could. She was to the IDF what Bob Hope was to the American soldiers. She especially loved the paratroopers and

Sharon, who was instrumental in bringing her grandparents out of Yemen after the War of Independence.

That Friday evening was magical. Shoshana lit the Shabbat candles and sang nonstop for over two hours. At the end of the evening, she promised to come for Shabbat dinner whenever we were in camp – and she did. Sometimes we were away on maneuvers or on missions, but she kept her promise whenever we were at base.

Shoshana Damari

Sunday, we returned to our training routine. Things were also getting interesting at the borders. The loose bands of Fedayeens were getting organized, supported by the Arab countries with weapons and training. We had to make adjustments to our training. We started getting briefings from military intelligence about terrorist camps in Jordan, Egypt, Libya, Syria and the Bekaa Valley in Lebanon. The decision was made to start raiding camps in their host countries. The bulk of these raids were to be done by the paratroopers' recon unit where I served.

I was a Lieutenant, Second in Command of my recon company. However, a week after the first visit by Shoshana Damari, our entire brigade had a training jump in the Negev (southern Israel desert), at which time Capt. Dudu, the company commander, broke his leg. Consequently, I took over command of the company. I wasn't quite 19 years old.

Chapter 23

The Old Man

As I wrote before, we Israelis totally believed in Israel. Our country was still young, but there was optimism, patriotism and a love of country that was strongly held. No one embodied this idealism stronger than our Prime Minister, David Ben Gurion.

While I was recovering from a minor hand injury, five of my men and I had the privilege to serve as his bodyguards in Kibbutz Sde Bokar, where he and his doting wife, Paula, lived.

The "Old Man," or "BG," as everyone called him, liked to walk a total of 6 km every morning. I used to send four of my guys up ahead of us to make sure the road was clear. (On one occasion, we did capture three terrorists setting up an ambush in one of the caves).

BG was our leader. He had a way of focusing on a person, dazzling him, making him feel special. His mind burned with such intensity, it seemed to throw a spell over people. Even his most offhand comment seemed charged with hidden importance. He would shower a person with attention, treat them as if they were the most important person in the world. You'd have to experience it to understand.

Since I knew his grandson, Yariv, from being in the Officer's Academy together, I was invited to sit at the dinner table with the family on Fridays when they visited. (Yariv did not complete the program). I heard the ideology of my country expressed as only he could say it. "Israel has created a new image of the Jew in the world. The image of a working and intellectual people, of a people that can fight with heroism, and win."

Hearing his words, I rejoiced in knowing that I helped restore the dignity and glory of my people with the life I had chosen. It was 1960. I was 19 years old.

David Ben-Gurion, first Prime Minister of Israel

Our "soft duty" with BG only lasted two memorable weeks, then back to Tel Nof.

Chapter 24

Extra Curricular Activities

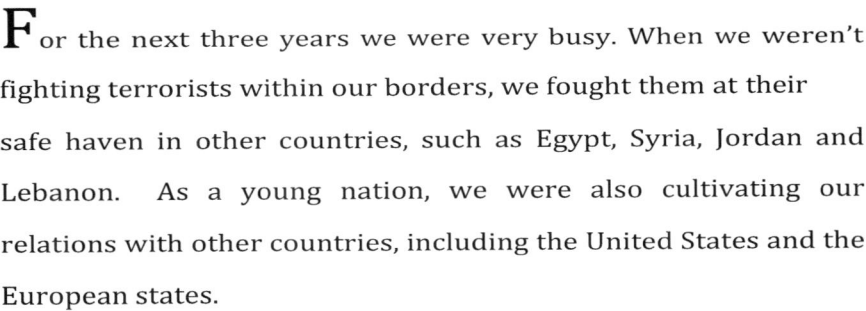

For the next three years we were very busy. When we weren't fighting terrorists within our borders, we fought them at their safe haven in other countries, such as Egypt, Syria, Jordan and Lebanon. As a young nation, we were also cultivating our relations with other countries, including the United States and the European states.

In 1960, I was involved in two such missions. The first mission involved four of my men and I sneaking into the Bekaa Valley in Lebanon—a very lawless part of the country loaded with terrorists and criminal gangs. We were asked to blow up a warehouse used as a facility to print counterfeit American dollars. It took us almost four hours at night to reach the warehouse undetected. We set the explosives with a two-hour timer, then hightailed it back to Israel. We didn't see the explosion, but were told the warehouse no longer existed.

My Name Was Alec. A Memoir by Allen Jacoby

The second mission, requested by a friendly country, was more complicated. We were asked to skydive into Libya, take photographs of a terrorist training camp, and exfiltrate with help from the navy. This was one of my most challenging missions, both physically and emotionally. A part of what continues to disturb my sleep.

A total of nine of us took off from Tel Nof at night: My friends Smolik, Tzveeka, David, and Yossi were among them. My friend Ari, was the jumpmaster. Smolik and David had special cameras. We were to do a high altitude, low opening jump from 12,000 feet, bury the chutes, walk to the camp about 2 km away, hide and take pictures for two days. Afterwards, we were to retrieve our chutes, walk about 8 km to the ocean, get picked up by a PT boat that would take us 12 km to a waiting navy boat, and finally back to home.

At 1:00 a.m., we got over the target. I was standing at the door looking at Ari when he pointed. I was out the door. Immediately, I fell for 70 seconds, yanked the handle, and watched the main chute billow out overhead. My speed dropped from 120 to 20 mph. The noise of the airplane's engines and the whistling rush of the wind disappeared. Everything was silent. The stars spread out above like diamonds over a black blanket. I looked down and the landscape below looked peaceful and, more importantly, empty.

Within 5 minutes after landing, our chutes were buried and we headed west. In 15 minutes we found a small hill overlooking the camp. We saw about 15 tents. It was 4:00 am; there was no activity except for two guards walking the perimeter. We got settled on the hill with Smolik and David facing the camp with their cameras. I'm between them with binoculars. Tzveeka and Yossi are about 100 yards behind us facing the other way.

At daylight the camp came alive. There were men, women, and a few children – about 82 people in total. Most of them looked Middle Eastern, but there were about 6 who looked Asian and maybe 9 Westerners. We assumed the Westerners were from the IRA. They all had weapons – mostly AK-47's.

In the middle of the camp was a concrete platform, 4 feet high, 10 feet long and 8 feet wide, with four hooks embedded in the concrete – two on each end. We had no idea what was its purpose.

The first day passed slowly with not much activity. We took turns sliding backwards from the hill to drink, eat, and pee. The next morning everything was the same until 9:00 am, when a jeep arrived. Two men got out and dragged a young man from the back seat. He looked Middle Eastern. His face was bloodied and swollen. By that time, the camp was alive with people jumping around, excited and yelling. A man came out from the middle tent and talked to the two new arrivals. They dragged the young man to the concrete platform. When they ripped off all of his clothes, we saw many cuts and bruises all over his body. They proceeded to lay him on the concrete slab, spread eagle, and tied his hands and legs to the four hooks.

The camp leader pointed to two women who approached the platform. One had a long knife and the other proceeded to put a few folded rags and towels under his head.

While I was still trying to figure out what was going on, the woman with the knife stepped on a stool next to the platform. With one quick motion, she plunged the knife into his groin and, in an upward motion, sliced him open to his sternum. The man was screaming. The three of us were in shock. It wasn't over. The woman dropped the knife, put her hands in the open cavity and pulled out his intestines and organs, then laid them on his chest. Now we understood why the towels were placed under his head. The young man was screaming and banging his head, but the towels softened his blows, keeping him conscious as he bled out.

While this was going on, the camp was in a wild frenzy, screaming, dancing and shooting their guns – men, women and children. The three of us on the hill felt sick. How could humans do something like this? "What kind of animals are these?" I whispered to Smolik. He looked at me with tears in his eyes. I looked at David and he, too, was crying. I wiped my tears and put my head down.

At nightfall, we retreated from the hill, picked up our chutes, and headed to the ocean. We got picked up by the PT boat and headed home. After debriefing, we handed over the cameras. Yossi and Tzveeka headed to the barracks. They hadn't seen what happened. Smolik, David and I headed for the tent.

Yechiel (middle) and company returned safely from Libya.

Chapter 25

When in Rome...

We didn't sleep that night in the tent after what we saw in Libya. I remember David asking if the fighting will ever stop. "I don't know," I said. "We can only hope, but I heard someone say in the academy that 'peace is that fleeting moment in history when the human race stops to reload.'" "That's depressing," David said. Smolik said, "I heard someone asking Einstein, 'What kind of weapons will be used in World War III?' and he said, 'I don't know, but World War IV will be fought with sticks and stones.'"

We kept talking the whole night. At 6:00 a.m. Yaki came in and told me I was needed in the briefing room. When I went into the meeting, I saw the camp's intelligence officer (my old friend, Rivka), and another civilian. Rivka proceeded to introduce me to Rafi Eitan, the Director of Operations for Mossad. We shook hands and he wasted no time explaining our next mission.

My Name Was Alec. A Memoir by Allen Jacoby

The Mossad had captured Adolf Eichmann in Argentina and smuggled him into Israel to stand trial for Crimes Against Humanity. Eichmann had been in charge of dealing with the "Jewish Problem," resulting in the murder of six million Jews. Utilizing gas chambers and other unspeakable measures in the various death camps across Europe, about half of all the Jewish people in the world were exterminated. Rafi wanted us to find out how Eichmann, and other Nazis, managed to get out of Europe after the war, settling in countries in South America and the Middle East.

The Mossad knew that Eichmann was captured by the Americans, and had escaped from prison, probably with inside help. He was possibly seen in Rome, but then disappeared until he was spotted again in Argentina. Rafi said they had information that the Red Cross was involved. Rivka was heading a team to Rome under diplomatic cover. They wanted me to meet them there to afford them protection. Since I used to be a competitive swimmer, I could tag along as a substitute swimmer with the Israeli team at Rome's 1960 Olympics. He asked if I had any questions. I said, "Yes. When do I leave?" He smiled and said, "Next week."

We arrived in Rome on a Thursday. I rode the bus to the Olympic Village, changed my clothes, and got a ride to the embassy, where I met Rivka and other Mossad members.

The next three days I was bored as Rivka and her crew poured over documents. Finally, by noon on Sunday, Rivka told me that they found a connection between a Red Cross office, a Catholic Church, and a high Nazi official located in Syria.

We needed to get into the building containing the Red Cross office. I asked the head of security at the embassy for two men, three walkie-talkies, and a car, which he agreed to right away. Ten minutes later, the three of us drove to the location of the Red Cross building. It turned out that the building and the church were practically across the street from each other. We drove around the neighborhood to get a feel for the place before returning to the embassy. We met with Rivka's crew and explained the situation. I told them we would leave at 1:00 a.m. They would split up into two units – two Mossad and one Embassy person each. I would remain outside to watch the car and make sure they were not interrupted. We had to be done by 4:30 a.m.

The mission went off like clockwork. By 9:00 a.m., we were on a flight back to Israel. Rivka dropped me off at the Tel Nof camp and promised to let me know what they got as soon as they developed the films and deciphered all the information.

She did. It turned out that the church had been hiding the Nazis and making arrangements in different host countries for them.

They also located their families and moved them to the new countries as well. The Red Cross supplied new Red Cross I.D.'s and passports, and transported them on what became known as the "Rat Line." I looked at Rivka and asked, "What the hell is wrong with these people? Why do they hate us?" We had no logical answer.

Israel could do nothing about the Red Cross, or the Catholic Church, but that little mission got us a lot of names and locations of Nazi hideouts. Mossad agents were kept busy for quite a while. But there would be no more trials.

In Rome. Yechiel with Rivka (left) and a member of Mossad team.

Chapter 26

More Family History

After returning from Rome, I got a three-day pass and a ride to Haifa. My family was moving to America. I was going to say goodbye. Since I ran away from home when I was 14 years old, I came to Haifa whenever I could, but never to my parents' house. I saw Pop and my brother, Shaya, a few times, but mostly I visited friends and cousins, especially my cousin Malka and her boyfriend, David. I usually slept at my Uncle Zalman's house. His family lived by the beach in Haifa. They had a long porch facing the ocean and he used half of it to make a bedroom for me with glassed in out-facing walls. I loved watching and listening to the Mediterranean.

This trip to Haifa to say goodbye brought me mixed feelings. I loved Pop and my brothers, but I never resolved my issues with my mother. I didn't love, respect or even like her. She was a selfish, self-centered person. The way she abused Pop, her children, and the rest of the family was ugly and unforgivable. I did not know how to deal with my feelings, and had no one to help me deal with them, so I tried never to think of her. Sometimes, when I saw my friends and cousins with their mothers, I felt conflicted – even jealous.

This was one of those times. I was sad to see Pop and my brothers leave, but glad to have my mother gone. We took some family pictures, said goodbye, and I watched the ship sail out to sea, hoping my brothers would come back some day.

By the time I got back to my uncle's house it was dinner time. He and I sat on the porch watching and listening to the sea.

After a while I asked him, since he was a friend to both, to tell me more about my biological father and Pop. He told me that his parents (my grandparents) lived in a small town in Poland. He was one of their six children – three boys and three girls. My grandfather was a very smart and careful man, such that in 1939 he decided that Poland was not a safe place for Jews and moved the entire family to Russia. He was, of course, correct as Poland was the first country conquered by Germany.

Zalman and his brothers had worked as carpenters. My grandparents were bakers. Misha, my biological father, lived with his uncle not far from our family, while he attended university. The rest of Misha's family lived in Ukraine. Zalman and Misha became friends and, sometimes, Misha was invited for

Shabbat dinner. That was how he met my mother. At the end of 1939, they got married and moved to Ukraine to live with his family.

By that time, World War II was in full swing. Misha and most other young men were drafted to fight the invading Germans. Word got back that Misha had been killed. Zalman didn't know what happened to his family, but my mother, who was pregnant, managed to get on a train heading to Russia. It took her two months to get to the family. I was born along the way. Most details from that time are very sketchy.

By the end of 1942, the war was raging in Europe and Zalman joined a small partisan group famously headed by the two Bielski brothers (watch the 2008 film, "Defiance"). They roamed the forest, trying to save as many Jewish people as possible. One day they found two Polish soldiers. They were in terrible shape and one had a bullet in his shoulder. Luckily, one of the partisans was a doctor and he removed the bullet. Zalman described how they nursed them back to life and discovered they were Jewish cousins from a city in Poland called Lodz. Lodz was the second-largest city in Poland, and a third of its population had been Jewish. In 1940, the Germans herded 164,000 Jews into the Lodz Ghetto. When the Russians liberated the ghetto, they found only 877 Jewish survivors.

The cousins had been captured by the invading Germans, but escaped one night with Isaac (Ike) getting shot. Zalman and Ike became friends and, in 1943 when Zalman decided to return to his family, he brought Ike with him. That's when Ike met my mother. They got married, and he became my father.

Later on, Ike learned that, with the exception of a few cousins who escaped to South Africa, his entire family perished in the ghetto. Ike's older brother, who was in France when the war broke out, survived the war. But at the end, some survivors commandeered a German boat and tried to cross the English Channel. They were sunk by the RAF who mistook them for Nazis. They all perished, except for the one survivor, who told the story.

Zalman told me that Ike was the best man he ever knew: kind, humble, unassuming and generous. He told me that Ike loved me very much and was very proud of me. "So am I," he said. "I know," I said. "I love him too and I love you as well." He stood up, kissed me on my head and went to bed. I stayed up on the porch the rest of the night, thinking about how lucky I was. At 19, I had already lived a lifetime that others take a whole lifetime to live.

After breakfast, I kissed my uncle, aunt, and three cousins, then hitched a ride to Neve Eitan to visit with my old friends. We had lunch and took a dip in the pool. My old swim coach, Avner, drove me back to Tel Nof.

The family as they left to live in USA. (Left to right: Ben, Yechiel, Ezra, Mother, Pop, Shaya)

Chapter 27

My Purpose

I got back to Tel Nof late in the afternoon. The first thing I saw was my company in full gear being addressed by Yaki. When they saw me, I heard a lot of "Hi Captain" and "Hi Yechi." I thought 'no officer in any army gets this kind of welcome.' So I asked Yaki what he was up to. He said they were going on a 10k run. I told him to give me 10 minutes to change. "I'm coming with you." He turned to the men and told them, "Take 10. Yechi missed us. He's going to change." I already felt better.

Yaki was in the lead. I stayed in back watching my guys. I realized how much I loved them. They were hardly different from each other, but different from other people in ways I admired. We weren't big guys, like badass football linemen, or like Rambo, but we could carry a 100-lb. pack, four hundred rounds and a machine gun, uphill, at a run. We were wolves, lean and mean. You did not want us on your ass. We were dangerous. I loved being part of the company. I couldn't think of anything I would rather be.

When we got back, my other sergeant, Zveeka, was waiting by the gate with big vats of warm water, towels and clean socks. He made all of us take off our shoes and socks, dip our feet in the water, and put on new socks.

After dinner, my guys built a fire outside, brewed coffee and told tall stories. In the meantime, I was in the Base Commander's office getting briefed for our next mission. I didn't want that life to ever end.

Chapter 28

Conundrum

Between September 1960 and March 1961, life was pretty normal. We trained hard and had a few missions, mostly ambushes, and some raids into Jordan and Egypt to capture terrorists, with intelligence provided by Mossad or MI (Military Intelligence). My company had a few injuries, mostly from training and parachute jumps, but no fatalities.

One of the missions into a small village in Gaza was especially memorable. We found our target asleep in a tent and picked him up without a fight. As we were leaving, I was approached by the village Mukhtar (village chief). He asked me to have coffee with him, so Smolik, (who spoke better Arabic) and I sat down on the ground by the fire next to his hut. He poured coffee into three fenjans (small coffee cups without handles) and talked about Middle East problems. Of course, we didn't solve anything, but I remember asking him why they hated us so much. I told him there is so much room in the Middle East and that most of the land is occupied by over 100 million Arabs. We 5 million Israelis occupy such a small area. Without missing a beat, he said, "But you are racists. You discriminate against us." I replied, "That's not true. We respect all the inhabitants of this land. Why would you think we are racist?" "Because we had many military conflicts, usually won by you, but you never raped our women," he retorted. I looked at Smolik. He shrugged his shoulders and said, "I've heard this before." Without a response, we thanked our host for the coffee and left.

When we got back to our base, I went to Sharon's office and told him what happened. "How do you answer a statement like that?" I asked. He said that he had also heard it before. He said, if you deny, they don't believe you. If you don't answer, they see it as proof that it's true. If you deny and say that it's immoral, they will say that you are holding yourself above them as a more moral and enlightened people. "If I knew the answer," he said, "I would win the Nobel prize." I looked at him for a moment and remarked, "Then there is no end in sight, is there?" "Maybe not in sight," he said, "but the title of our national anthem is 'Hope'. Don't lose it."

Chapter 29

Israel's Bar Mitzvah

In April 1961, I was picked to lead the paratroopers for the four-day march celebrating Israel's Independence Day. That year was the 13th anniversary (Bar Mitzvah) of the rebirth of Israel in our ancient homeland. Every year we have weeklong activities that include parties, speeches, barbecues and dinners. By far, the most inclusive and popular activity was the 4-Day March, culminating with a parade in our capital, Jerusalem. Every branch of the military was represented, and the participants were judged along the route for speed, endurance, and synchronized marching by selected judges from headquarters. Civilians also participated, either in groups made up of sports teams and schools, or individually.

The winning team was picked on the fourth day in Jerusalem. I felt extremely honored to be picked to lead the unit representing the storied 202nd Paratroopers' Brigade – arguably the best in the IDF. This was most special as it was our 13th anniversary –

a young country's soldiers led by the youngest graduate from the officers' academy.

On May 11th, all participants assembled at the staging area. We arrived in the afternoon. First, most of our brigade made a regular parachute jump into the staging area. It was impressive to watch 120 chutes deploy. After they landed, my 36-member team and I skydived from 8,000 feet, deploying our chutes after free-falling for 7,200 feet. Very impressive. But after landing, I looked at the faces of the people on the ground and knew something was wrong. Yaki, who was in the group that jumped first, came over and told us that two men got their chutes tangled in the high tension electric lines and, before they were able to untangle, a gust of wind re-inflated the canopies. Their helmets hit the electric wires and both died.

We were in shock and felt paralyzed. It's bad enough to lose someone in combat, but this incident was almost too much to bear. Sharon gathered us around him and somehow managed to impress upon us that, despite what happened, it was still the country's birthday and we still had a mission. We got ourselves together and prepared for the march the next morning.

That day, we got up early and took off running the first 20 km. At the marker, two of my sergeants, Yaki and Smolik, waited for us with clean shirts. After changing shirts, we lined in parade formation and marched back to the staging area. By that time, the rest of the participants started on their first 20 km, looking at us with surprise as we were already on our way back. We saw a couple of judges making note and smiling. There was nothing in the rules about running, so for the next two days we repeated the same tactic.

On the fourth and final day, we had to walk the full 40 km from the staging area to Jerusalem. We got up early, shaved, polished our boots, put on new uniforms, utility belts, took our Uzi submachine guns and lined up in parade formation. I inspected my men. We looked great. I reminded them that today we would take it easy. We would let all the other military units get ahead of us. We knew that we were the main attraction and I wanted the anticipation to build.

The minute we stepped onto Ben Yehuda Street (the main street in Jerusalem), the crowds went crazy. Kids were hoisted on their parents' shoulders, teenagers were jumping up and down and yelling "Tzanhanim," ("paratroopers" in Hebrew), over and over. We won first place unanimously.

Two weeks later, the military magazine "Bamahane" (meaning "in the camp") was published. On the cover were photos of six young outstanding IDF officers. My picture was among them.

Yechiel leading his troops into Jerusalem on Israel's Bar Mitzvah.

Yechiel on the cover of "Bamahane"

Chapter 30

Revenge Interruptus

T hough we were elated to win first place in the 4-Day March, the memory of that triumphant week would always remain bittersweet when recalling the price two men paid.

After that week, Shoshana Damari was coming once again to sing for us on Shabbat. Normally, when the first star in the sky is visible, Shabbat officially begins with the lighting of the candles. However, that day we experienced the worst storm of the year: pouring rain, lightning and thunder. We couldn't see any stars that night, so Shoshana lit the candles at 7:00 pm and we had our favorite dinner of fried chicken and french fries around 9:00 pm.

The sergeant on duty in our office came in and walked over to where Sharon and the base commander were sitting, whispering to them. We knew something was wrong when I saw Sharon look directly at me. He stood up and said, "We don't have all the details, but there was a terrorist infiltration and shooting in a kibbutz near the Jordan River." He then turned to me and said, "Yechi, have your sergeant get your company ready. You grab a couple of guys and a driver. Get to Neve Eitan as quickly as you can and report back. " My stomach clenched. Neve Eitan was the kibbutz where I spent three years of my life, after running away from home at the age of 14.

I immediately told Yaki to get the company ready to move. Then I asked Smolik to get three guys, a command car and driver, and to meet me by the flagpole in 15 minutes. I ran to the barracks, grabbed my "go gear" and headed to the flagpole. The Recon Unit always had a "go gear" ready that included a utility belt, weapons, and a backpack loaded with extra energy bars and other items to sustain us for a couple of days.

Within 15 minutes, Smolik, David, Yossi and I were on the road. At 10 00pm, we pulled up to the gate at Neve Eitan where two armed guards stood. I asked them where I could find Yaakov, the Kibbutz Secretary. They said that everyone was at the nursery. I gave our driver directions.

When I lived here, one of my jobs was milking the cows. I especially loved the night shift because we were usually done by 11:30 pm, and would head to the nursery where two of the nurses took care of the Kibbutz toddlers. They used to make us fried chicken and fries for a late dinner.

My Name Was Alec. A Memoir by Allen Jacoby

As we pulled up to the nursery, we saw a crowd of people standing outside in the pouring rain. I asked Smolik to come in with me. Inside I saw Yaakov talking to the two nurses and, as usual, they were armed. On the floor to my left, I saw a dead terrorist. To my right on the floor, I saw Avner, my old swimming coach, and his wife holding each other and crying. I asked Yaakov what happened. He said I should speak to Yael and Hana, the nurses. I noticed then that there were no children in the nursery. Yael told me that the parents had picked them up.

Yael told me what happened: "Because of the storm, the kids were scared and crying around 8:30. I was holding Sara, Avner's daughter, trying to calm her down. Hana was in the back of the room rocking a cradle when suddenly, the door burst open and two guys with rifles burst in. One of them pointed the gun at me and took a shot, but hit Sara. Hana shot from back there and killed this one on the floor. The guy who shot Sara ran away." I checked the dead guy and he had three bullet holes in his chest. "Where is Sara?" I asked her. She walked over to the bed under the window and lifted the sheet. I saw Sara with a bullet hole in her forehead. She was 5 years old. The last time I saw her she was 2. I couldn't control myself and started crying. Smolik was standing next to me with tears running down his face. When I managed to regain my control, I told Smolik to wait for me outside with the guys. I walked over to Avner and his wife, hugged them hard, and walked out.

I gathered everyone under an awning and told them what happened. Then I explained what I planned to do. The one terrorist that ran away was going to try to cross the Jordan River back to Jordan. He would use one narrow dirt road where the deer came to drink from the river, and the Fedayeen sometimes used. It was about 2 km north. In this weather, the river was raging, so I figured he probably wouldn't try at that time. As the rain let up, he would probably try before daybreak.

I told the driver to take us up to that spot and drive back to Neve Eitan. I told him to call the base and tell them what we intended to do. When the mission was complete, we would call him on his walkie-talkie to come get us.

We were dropped off 1 km past the dirt road. After the driver left, we hiked to the river. We dropped back down to the dirt road where it met the river. I told Smolik to take the three men 100 yards back from the river and find shelter on both sides of the road. I stayed by the river, behind a tree.

It was 1:30 am, the rain had stopped. At 4 am, I heard a crack, like a branch snapping. By then, the clouds had cleared and the moon was out. I peeked from behind the tree and saw a guy holding a rifle with both hands, creeping along the path towards me. My right hand clenched, my senses sharpened, and I felt the adrenaline surging into my system. I felt a strange, indescribable emotion. Right then, I knew that this was why I was in this unit: to protect; failing that, to avenge.

He was almost at my tree. I stepped out and rammed the butt of my Uzi into his nose. I felt the bone give way. He dropped the rifle, his hands rose to his face, red blood spurting through his fingers. I pushed forward and buried the barrel into his stomach. It folded him in half. While he was doubled over, I drew the Uzi back and up to my shoulder, then chopped down against the back of his skull. He went face down into the mud, out like a light. This was all done without thinking, thanks to our training. I turned the Uzi around, pointing it at his head. Suddenly I heard Smolik say, "No, Yechi!" I looked up and saw my guys in front of me. "He is only an instrument, Yechi. The Mossad may be able to get the names of his handlers." With that, I snapped out of "the zone."

We tied his hands and dragged him out to the highway to wait for our truck. On the way back to camp, we stopped at Neve Eitan. Yaakov came out, looked at the terrorist and said he would tell Avner.

We got back to camp and turned the terrorist over to the M.P.'s. I headed straight for the tent, knowing that there would be no sleep for me that night.

Chapter 31

The Best Therapy

As predicted, there was no sleeping that night. At 6 am, Yaki came over leaving coffee and egg sandwiches. I drank the coffee while thinking of my time in Neve Eitan. How I met Avner and his brother at the pool. I reviewed swim tournaments we won and lost. I remembered when Sara was born. Three other babies were born around the same time – one boy and three girls. We had a party for the four of them, and the boy was circumcised. Everyone was so happy eating, drinking, singing and dancing.

Now, this beautiful 5-year-old was cut down before her life could truly begin. How many more will die? Will it ever be over? The only proverbial light I saw at the end of the tunnel was of a train coming the other way.

We can't give up hope. Hope is our national anthem and "Shalom" doesn't just mean hello or goodbye; it also means "peace." We just need good leaders. Until then we must be strong, so we were.

I looked at my watch, it was noon, so I decided to do some pushups. Before I could start I heard, "Anybody home?" I looked up and saw my two friends from Haifa, Rivka (now a Mossad agent) and Meir (now a Military Intelligence agent). We hugged and kissed. "What are you guys doing here?" I asked. Meir answered that Rivka had called him about what had happened in Neve Eitan, so they decided to drop by.

We reminisced about our school days – how we met in that first class. How we used to climb Mt. Carmel with slingshots, potatoes and matches to catch pigeons, barbecue and tell stories. We talked about how we stole a chicken, and how I wound up spending the night in jail. Meir pulled out a sock filled with marbles and said "let's play." I made a circle on the dirt floor and we played, just like when we were kids.

Meir told me that his mother and sister now lived in Jerusalem. "Remember when you bloodied my nose and my mother screamed at you? Well, she was watching the Independence Day parade and saw you leading the Paratroopers. She asked me to tell you she forgives you, and she wants to make dinner for us."

We spent most of the day talking and laughing. It was the best therapy. After they went home, I left the tent and rejoined my company.

Chapter 32

Talfiq

1961 passed with few changes in our routine. We trained hard, engaged in small missions tracking down infiltrators and setting up ambushes. Thankfully, we suffered no casualties or injuries. Shoshana Damari came to our camp on Fridays to sing. Life was good.

Yaki, Tzveeka and Smolik were all upgraded to First Sergeant. I was upgraded to Captain and a new young lieutenant joined the company as my second-in-command.

At the end of December, some of us attended a New Year's party at the American Embassy in Tel Aviv.

During the second week of 1962, we started planning a major raid into Egyptian territory in Gaza. It would be major for us because I was to use my entire company. Over the previous year, Palestinian terrorists had increased their infiltrations into Israel, causing not only a lot of property damage but, more importantly, they managed to kill two civilians and injure a few others. Most of this activity seemed to originate from Gaza. Military Intelligence had information that the terrorists had set up headquarters in a fortified police complex near the hillside village of Talfiq, aided by the Egyptians.

Our mission was to attack a fortified hill north of the village manned by a Fedayeen platoon. At the same time, we were to attack the police compound south of the village, destroy both targets and, importantly, remove the contents of a safe in the police station. The police station, we were told, had about ten men guarding it.

Based on the intelligence, I decided to use Joshua's tactic when he captured the city of Ai from the Canaanites (the same one I used as a cadet in the officer's academy to capture Mt. Tabor in a training exercise). The plan was for us to cross into Gaza at 2 am. My new second-in-command would stop at the hill north of the village with the 3rd platoon. Tzveeka, with the 2nd platoon, would set up halfway between the hill and the police station. I would lead the 1st platoon, setting up by the police station. We were to be at our locations by 3:30 am. At 4 am, the 3rd platoon would attack the hill. When the guards in the police compound headed out to help their buddies on the hill, Tzveeka, with the 2nd platoon, would ambush them on the road.

At exactly 4 am, we heard the shooting from the hill. Within five minutes, we watched a truck speed out of the police yard with about half a dozen men in the bed. Two guys armed with AK-47's remained on guard at the yard entrance. We were about 75 yards away, so Smolik and I took them down with two clean shots. Then the eight of us walked in with no opposition. Yaki placed four men as guards. He and David started placing the explosives around the building while Smolik and I went inside to open the safe. Smolik placed an explosive shaped like a rope around the safe's door and lit the 30-second fuse. We took cover while the explosives worked perfectly. We took everything out of the safe, put it in a backpack and ran out to pick up Yaki and his men. Smolik lit a 2-minute fuse for the explosives around the building before we hightailed it out of there.

We got about 200 yards away when Smolik, who was watching our backs, hollered "'Indians,' (meaning enemies). Take cover!" We all dropped to the ground. I looked back and saw an entire Egyptian company of about 72 men spreading out in attack formation. I asked Smolik, "How long?" "Forty seconds," he replied. So I told the men to stay down until the building blew. "Then we move through the village using the buildings for cover." I told the radioman to check with Tzveeka, to learn their location. They had already crossed the border back into Israel.

Just then, the police building exploded. The Egyptians were not expecting it and took cover. We then started "leap-frogging" out of there. Yaki and three men ran back for cover while my three men and I fired at the Egyptians. When they reached cover, they stopped and opened fire to give us cover to leap-frog past them. We almost made it.

Twenty yards from the border, Yaki's group got up to leap-frog my group and I heard someone yell, "Yaki is hit!" I looked around. We were at the border with my men and Yaki's men. I looked back and saw Yaki about 70 yards away on his back. I grabbed the binoculars. The Egyptians were behind cover of the buildings about 20 yards from Yaki. I saw that he took an RPG (a rocket propelled grenade) in the stomach. It is usually fired at a group – not an individual. The damage it caused was devastating. I could see that Yaki's guts were blown out, but he was still moving his leg. I didn't know if he was alive or if nerves were moving his leg. The Egyptians were sniping him, hoping that we would try to retrieve him. I could see that he was going to die, if he wasn't dead already. If we left him behind and he was still alive, they would torture him before he died.

Smolik put his hand on my shoulder and said, "Go take care of the men, Yechi. I'll do this." I looked at him and said, "No, it's my responsibility. Get back. I'll join you soon."

I tried to remain calm. I knew that I couldn't break down in front of the men – and in enemy territory, but I kept tearing up. My heart was pained, and my mind kept going back to basic training. We were the Four Musketeers – Ari, Tzveeka, Yaki and I. Ari became a jumpmaster, but he was also based in Tel Nof and we saw him often. Tzveeka, Yaki and I had been inseparable for the past four years. Training, missions, dinner with their families – especially at Yaki's grandmother's home. We were brothers— closer than brothers because of what we shared. How could this happen?

Yaki was laying with his legs towards Egypt and his head toward Israel. I knew what I had to do, but my hands were shaking and my vision was blurry. I told myself to get it together. A shot like this is not easy, and I would only get one shot, so I did what all combat soldiers are trained to do. It's called "4x4x4 breath." It's counting breaths: breathe in to the count of 4, hold breath counting to 4, and let breath out to the count of 4. I repeated this until my hands were steadied. I sighted my Uzi on Yaki's head and pulled the trigger.

I crawled back to my men. We got on the trucks and headed back to Tel Nof. No one was talking. Most were crying. It was January 28, 1962. My sleep would never be peaceful again.

Chapter 33

Mourning

We returned to the base without talking. I went straight to the commanding officer and gave him a verbal report. He listened quietly, and when I finished he said, "I am going to see Arik [Sharon]." I nodded and told him that I would be in the Tent.

Ten minutes later, Tzveeka, Smolik and Ari came in with coffee. Ari told me to take a look outside, so I stepped out and saw my entire company sitting on the ground.

The day went by slowly. They took shifts bringing in drinks and food. The four of us spent the time reminiscing about Yaki. "Yaki was such a mother hen," said Ari. "Remember the 20k hike we had with full gear at night? Yaki stayed behind at the base, but when we got back, he was waiting at the gate with two guys who brought pails of warm water and clean socks. He made everyone take off their boots and socks, soak our feet in the warm water, and then put on the new socks." We nodded our heads with tears in our eyes.

"Remember when we trained 700 soldiers from Ghana?" I asked. "One morning at roll call, one of the soldiers moved and their sergeant walked up to him and slapped him across the face. Yaki nearly lost it. He grabbed the sergeant by the neck and told him if he ever slaps a soldier again he would cut his balls off."

Yes. Yaki was a great soldier, and an even better human being. Israel lost one of its best.

There were a lot of tears shed in Tel Nof that night from the eyes of some of the toughest soldiers in the world.

Chapter 34

The Value of a Life

At 7 pm, our commanding officer came into the tent and told me that officers from headquarters would be at the base at 1 pm tomorrow. I should be in the briefing room by 12:45, in dress uniform. I went outside and told my men to go back to the barracks, clean their weapons and themselves, and get some rest. Tzveeka, Ari and Smolik stayed with me in the tent.

The next morning, I cleaned my weapons, showered, shaved and put on my dress uniform. As I walked to the briefing room at the allotted time, I again saw my entire company outside, all clean and in their dress uniforms. I was so proud of my men. I felt my heart speed up and tears form again in my eyes.

Inside, I saw Arik Sharon, my commanding officer, and four officers from headquarters: two Generals, one Colonel and one Major. I knew one of the Generals because he was the commanding officer of the Academy. Arik told me to grab a coffee and come back at 3:00; they were going to talk to Tzveeka, Smolik and Lt. Yosi, my second in command. I would be last.

When I returned, they had three questions: (1) "Did you know that an Egyptian company was in the area?" "No, sir," I answered. (2) "Was Yaki dead or alive when you took the shot?" "I don't know," I replied. (3) "In hindsight, do you think there was a chance to retrieve the body?" "No, sir," was my answer.

The general in command looked at me, then said, "We are satisfied that you acted properly. As a matter of fact, the operation was very successful, even though the cost of life is painful. We are already in negotiations with Egypt, and expect Yaki's body may be back in Israel by tomorrow. Funeral arrangements will be coordinated with his family. They have asked me to give you time off to visit with them in Jerusalem. Take all the time you need."

An hour later, my commanding officer gave me his jeep and driver, and allowed me to take Tzveeka and Ari with me. We left for Jerusalem, to Yaki's grandmother's home.

We arrived in the late afternoon. At Yaki's grandmother's house were his entire family – parents, uncle, aunt, cousins. We all hugged and kissed and cried. In the living room was a long table with enough food to feed an army. "The neighbors and friends," Yaki's grandmother explained. Yaki's father said, "I talked to your commanding officer. He told me what happened. We don't want you to feel guilty. We know that the four of you were like brothers. It's just so unfair – surviving the Holocaust only to be killed in Israel."

We were silent for a while, when his grandmother said, "You know if it was meant to be – and I believe that everything is preordained. Dying defending your country and your people is better than being put in the ovens by the Nazis."

Just then there was a knock on the door. Our driver came in and told us that he was on his way back when he got a call on his radio. They wanted me to call the base commander. When I did, I was told that a deal brokered with Egypt by the U.N. We were to turn over 22 POW's (prisoners-of-war) for Yaki's body at sunrise the next morning. After doctors examined Yaki's body, the funeral would take place on Friday. The commanding officer wanted me to handle the exchange. I asked if I could tell the family, and he agreed. I told everyone what happened. We said our goodbyes, and headed back to Tel Nof.

On our way back, our driver asked me why we made such a bad deal: "One body for 22 soldiers". I looked at him and said, "You are right. It was a bad deal. For the Egyptians. One of our people is priceless. They could have asked for 100 soldiers, and it still would be a bad deal for them. What is bad for us is that one of our young warriors is dead."

When we got back to the base, he thanked me for setting him straight: "I will never forget."

Chapter 35

The Exchange

It was very hectic when we got back. We had to take off within two hours to be at the Gaza border by 5 am. I met with my commanding officers, Dov and Sharon. They told me that the MP's were on the way escorting a truck with the 22 prisoners then asked me what I needed. I told them I needed a command car with a driver, and a coffin. I also told them I wanted to take Ari, Smolik and Tzveeka with me. Arik (Sharon) said OK, and to stay in touch with them by radio.

We ran to our barracks, showered, shaved, and put on our dress uniforms. By the time we got back outside, the MP's, prisoners, and our command car were waiting by the gate. We took off, with the prisoners and MP's following behind.

Arriving at the crossing by 4:45 am, they were waiting for us: three UN Blue Helmets led by a Major, a platoon of Egyptian soldiers led by a Captain, and an empty truck. Yaki's body was on the bed of the truck, wrapped in a blanket. I told the MP Sergeant to turn over the prisoners. Tzveeka, Ari, Smolik and I unwrapped Yaki, and gently put him in our coffin before carrying it to the command car. I told the driver we were leaving.

While doing this, the Egyptians and UN soldiers saluted. I ignored them. We unfurled the flag over the coffin. I had Smolik and Ari sit on the left bench, Tzveeka and I sat on the right – all facing the coffin. I called the camp to tell them we were on our way. It was 5 am, and the slow drive would take about 3-1/2 hours. The first half-hour was through uninhabited terrain, then through small towns and villages. People stopped and stood at attention when we passed by.

We got to Tel Nof at 9 am. At the gate, the command car stopped. I looked over the cab in amazement. In front of the car stood Sharon with 12 other officers, and on both sides of the road stood the camp's entire personnel at attention: pilots, paratroopers, mechanics and all the support personnel. Sharon and his officers turned and started a slow walk to the infirmary. We followed him while the entire camp escorted us. At the infirmary, everyone stood at attention until we walked the coffin inside and handed Yaki over to the Base Doctor and his people.

I don't know how everyone felt on that Wednesday morning, but the four of us were drained. We walked out and sat on the ground, lighting cigarettes. Sharon came out and kneeled in front of us. I gave him a cigarette. He looked at us and asked how we were feeling. I told him, "I feel terrible. I lost one of the best friends I've ever had, but also, I feel pride. I'm so proud of our people. It's a strange feeling. It's like at the Seder on Passover. You eat something bitter and something sweet. I am bitter for losing Yaki, but I'm so proud to be part of the Jewish people and in Israel." He was quiet for a while, then said, "I will remember this."

Chapter 36

How are the Mighty Fallen!

At 8 am on Thursday, we all met in Sharon's office to hear the doctor's report. I only had one question: "Which shot killed Yaki?" "We can't tell," he said. "The RPG to the stomach, or the head shot were kill shots by themselves. He may have lived for a minute or two after the RPG, but definitely not longer. It is irrelevant. My report will say that the RPG killed Yaki." He went on to say, "I will also note that the head shot was taken to prevent possible suffering." To this day, part of me knows I did the right thing, yet part of me suffers from the guilt of having to do it.

Sharon informed us that the funeral would take place the next day, Friday, at 9 am in Jerusalem on the Mount of Olives where all paratroopers are buried. He told us that the entire company would escort Yaki to Jerusalem and asked that I prepare a short eulogy, and let him review it by the end of day. I asked him if I could make a quick run to Haifa to pick up my family's Torah scroll. He looked at me oddly and asked, "Your family has a Torah scroll?" "Yes," I said. "My grandfather's." "There must be a story behind it," he remarked. "There is," I said, "and I'll explain tomorrow." He told me to take his driver.

We got to Haifa at noon, and drove directly to the little synagogue where I had my Bar Mitzvah. This was where the Torah scroll was kept. I explained to the rabbi why I needed the scroll for the next two days. Ten minutes later we were on our way back to Tel Nof with the scroll in hand.

The next day, we all left camp at 6 am to go to Jerusalem. I met with Rabbi Goran and explained what I wanted to do, then handed him the scroll. He told me that at 11 am, there would be a short service at the pavilion, which is a large tent with open sides about a half-mile from the actual cemetery. After he completed his remarks, I would give the eulogy, then we would all walk to the grave site.

When my turn came to give the eulogy, I must admit I was nervous. I was looking at 200 people, including my entire company, Yaki's family and dignitaries. I performed my breathing exercises and began. First, I explained that I was speaking for the entire 202nd Brigade, especially for Yaki's and my company. Then, I explained the Torah scroll. This little scroll had belonged to my grandfather, who carried and cared for it as if it was the greatest treasure. He carried it from a little village in Poland, to Russia, to the Ukraine, always staying a step ahead of the Nazis. From the Ukraine, he carried it to a Displaced Persons Camp in Germany, where he had to discard all of his worldly goods, but never the Torah. From Germany to Italy, to Cypress, and finally home to the Holyland, Israel.

The scroll's history isn't much different than Yaakov's or mine, or thousands of other young men of my generation, who were lovingly and safely dragged across a war-torn Europe to our home, Israel. Now we are charged, and gladly accept our responsibility to defend our people and homeland. Some of our best gave their lives. Yaakov was one such man. To eulogize him, I read King David's lament for Prince Jonathan from this little scroll:

How are the mighty fallen!
Tell it not in Gath,
Publish it not in the streets of Ashkelon,
Lest the daughters of the Philistines rejoice;
Lest the daughters of the
Uncircumcised triumph.
Ye mountains of Gilboa,
Let there be no dew nor rain upon you,
Neither fields of choice fruits,

For there the shield of the mighty

Was vilely cast away.

From the blood of the slain,

From the fat of the mighty,

The bow of Jonathan turned not back

And the sword of Saul returned not empty.

Saul and Jonathan, the lovely

And the pleasant.

In their lives, even in their death,

They were not divided.

They were swifter than eagles;

They were stronger than lions.

Ye daughters of Israel, weep over them.

How are the mighty fallen in the midst of the battle.

Jonathan upon thy high places is slain!

I am distressed for thee, my brother Jonathan.

Wonderful was thy love to me.

How are the mighty fallen.

There wasn't a dry eye in the tent. And on that day, we buried my best friend.

Chapter 37

Stranger in Our Midst

After Yaki's funeral, I rushed to Haifa to return the Torah scroll before sunset (the beginning of Shabbat). I got back to Tel Nof before Shoshana lit the Shabbat candles. She had dinner with us, but there would be no singing after dinner that night.

I was told that Sunday morning, the entire brigade would be parachuting into the desert near the Salt Sea (aka the Dead Sea), to commence weeklong training maneuvers. We spent Saturday getting ready; cleaning and packing our equipment. I also spent time with the other commanders, reviewing maps, getting briefings on the scope of the exercise, and my company's responsibilities.

At 5 am on Sunday, my company boarded four helicopters and took off to the Salt Sea. Our assignment was to secure an area of four square miles. By 10 am, three planes arrived over the area we had prepared. The planes dropped three jeeps, two command cars and other heavy equipment, like mortars and cannons, with parachutes. At 1 pm, twelve Dakota and Nord airplanes flew over and dropped 400 paratroopers. It was an awesome sight to see, the sky full of deployed canopies. Even more amazing was that there were absolutely no injuries.

By 6 pm, we were ready. The tents were erected, equipment was tested, and we were good to go. We would start the maneuvers in coordination with other IDF units deployed in different locations. I cannot describe the kind of maneuvers we engaged in that week, but something very exciting happened to me personally.

On Monday night, after a very full and active day, we got back to camp around 6 pm, had dinner, and everyone crashed for a well-deserved night's sleep. Everyone but the officers. We stayed in the main tent for debriefing and planning the next day's activities. Finally at 10 pm, I crawled back into my tent and fell asleep in about ten seconds.

Suddenly, I felt a hand shake my shoulder and someone call out, "Captain... Captain." I opened my eyes and saw one of my guys. I looked at him and said, annoyed, "I just fell asleep. What is it?" He said, "Yechi, it's 5 am. Someone is here to see you!" I looked at my watch. Shit! I slept seven hours! I crawled out of my tent and saw a civilian standing next to my guy. Must be Mossad, I thought. I asked the stranger if I could help him, and he put out his hand to shake mine. I shook it as he said, "Shalom, Alec. I am your cousin, Natan."

Chapter 38

My New Cousin

I looked at him. "I don't have a cousin named Natan," I said. He smiled, "Yes you do. I'm from South Africa, and two weeks ago I saw your family in Philadelphia." At that point, I heard someone say, "You guys need to talk," and for the first time I realized that Sharon was also there. Sharon informed me that my cousin was a Jewish hero and to take three days off, offering his driver.

I shook my head, looked at my 'cousin,' and told him I needed ten minutes. I found Yossi, my second in command, and told him to take command of the company. Then I went to find Tzveeka, to ask him to take care of my gear. I told him I'd see him Friday. My new cousin and I got into Sharon's car and took off for Tel Aviv. I thought perhaps he was related to my biological father, Misha, and as though he read my thoughts, Natan said, "You must wonder how we're related. Ike's father, your grandfather, and my father, were brothers." "Wow," I said. "It will take a while to get to Tel Aviv. Why don't you start from the beginning?"

"OK," he said. "Your father's family, and my family lived in Poland for generations. In 1933, when Hitler came to power in Germany, my father decided that Europe was not safe anymore so our side of the family moved to South Africa. Your grandfather's family stayed in Poland. Eventually, we learned that his entire family perished in the Holocaust — all except for your father. We settled in South Africa – my parents, brother and sister. My father opened a furrier shop, which I inherited when he passed away. We assumed the European branch of our family was gone."

"During the war, I served in the South African Air Force. In 1947, I volunteered as a pilot in Israel's War of Independence. When I returned from Israel, I worked with my father until he passed away. My brother became a doctor, and my sister, in her free time, started tracking down any surviving family members. In 1960, to everyone's surprise, she found a cousin in Haifa. His name was Victor. He was a butcher, and his mother was the sister of your grandfather and my father. On one of my trips to Europe, I detoured to Israel and found him. He told me that your father and he were in the Polish Army and had been captured by the Germans, but managed to escape. Both ended up in Haifa, but he told me that your father had moved to America. He had their address in Philadelphia, so two weeks ago when I was in

Philadelphia, I met your entire family. When your father told me he had a son who is an officer in the Israeli Paratroopers, I decided to come back and find you."

"So, how did you find me?" I asked. He responded by asking, "Do you know Moti Hod?" "Of course," I said. "He is Israel's Air Force. Without him, we wouldn't have an air force. Every time I make a jump, it is from an airplane piloted by one of his." Natan replied, "When I came here in 1947 as a volunteer pilot, he was in charge. We became good friends. When I came looking for you, I went to Tel Nof and told him why I was in Israel again. Moti said, 'If you are looking for an officer in the paratroopers, follow me,' and he took me to another office and introduced me to Sharon. I told Sharon I'm looking for one of his boys named Alec Yakobovich. He said he didn't know anyone by that exact name, but he did have a Yechiel Yakobovich. 'That's him,' I said. 'His Hebrew name is Yechiel, but his family still calls him Alec.' Sharon told me that the brigade was on maneuvers in the desert, but after Moti told him who I was, Sharon said he was about to leave to go there, and insisted I come with him. That's how I found you."

Natan was a great guy who loved to have fun. We spent two amazing days together in Tel Aviv and when I saw him off at the airport, he promised to come back to see me. Little did we know, the next time we would meet would be in Philadelphia.

Chapter 39

War and Peace

I got back to Tel Nof on Thursday night to an empty camp. The 202nd was scheduled to come back Friday morning. I had dinner with the pilots in their dining room, and played a few games of backgammon with one of them.

As is typical with Israelis, we got into a political debate and one of the pilots argued that we needed to make more sacrifices to achieve peace and reduce the military, thus saving money. Others argued that we would always need an army. One of the pilots turned to me. "What do you think, Yechi?"

I said I believed we would always need a strong military, especially if we wanted peace. "How do you figure that?" he asked. I told them that I once was Ben Gurion's bodyguard, and that he always liked to talk about war and peace. BG quoted the Greek philosopher, Plato (of course saying it first in Latin): "If you want peace, you must prepare for war." I agreed with BG that only a powerful army could deter our enemies.

I said goodnight and went to sleep. I got up early and went out for a run, but just as the sun slowly breached the horizon, I saw the trucks with my paratroopers rolling into base. I walked over to welcome my men. When my company disembarked, calling out my name, I felt happy and safe. My family was home.

Chapter 40

Future Assured

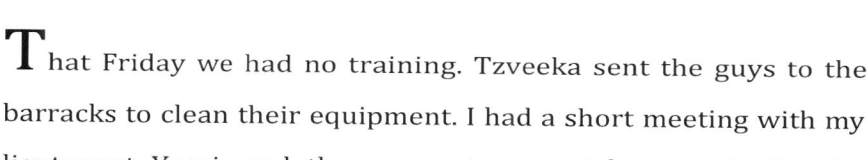

That Friday we had no training. Tzveeka sent the guys to the barracks to clean their equipment. I had a short meeting with my lieutenant Yossi, and the sergeants, to catch up and plan for Sunday.

At lunch, I was told to go see our commanding officer. When I got to his office, Sharon was there along with General Yitzhak Rabin, second in command to the Chief of Staff and in charge of personnel. Rabin would go on to serve two terms as Prime Minister and tragically be assassinated in 1995.

We discussed the two weeks of maneuvers. Rabin asked me if I planned to stay in the military. I told him that it was my life plan since I was 6 years old. "We make a big investment in our young officers. We want them to stay," he said. "I reviewed your record since you enlisted at 17. You are one of our youngest Captains. You will make Major in two years, and after that you will need a university degree to move up the chain of command. We will of course, pay for your education. Every year, we have a two-week course in advanced tactics for young officers. The next one starts Monday at headquarters in Tel Aviv. Be there Monday morning at 7 am. You will do great, but don't ever discuss what you learn there with anyone. I will see you tonight. Shoshana is coming."

That weekend was great. Shoshana was amazing. I spent the rest of Friday with my men. On Saturday, a few of us went down to the Kinneret (Sea of Galilee), and spent the day swimming and playing volleyball and racquetball. In the evening, we built a fire, ate shish kebobs, drank coffee and told tall tales. It was good to connect with my men.

We got back to camp around 2 am on Sunday, and at 5 am Monday, I got a ride to Tel Aviv, where I spent two weeks in a classroom. I don't know if the tactics we learned are still secret so I won't discuss them, but in short, they were war tactics.

After I completed the course, I decided to stop in Jerusalem, the 'City of Peace,' on my way back to Tel Nof. At the border separating the city into east and west, I saw Muslims, Jews and Christians in West Jerusalem. As a Jew, I was barred from crossing into East Jerusalem. I thought three religions worshiping the same God. You'd think He would be grateful, but instead He gives us all a hard time.

My Name Was Alec. A Memoir by Allen Jacoby

It was 1962. I was almost 21 years old, and my future was set. What could go wrong?

Chapter 41

Almost There

I left Jerusalem wondering how, in this city, there were so many plans made with so few results. I got out to the main road and hitched a ride with a young guy driving a small truck. "Where are you headed, soldier?" he asked. "Tel Nof," I said. He put out his hand and we shook. My name is Moti," he said, "I am an airplane mechanic. I served at Tel Nof. I'll take you there."

We spent the whole time talking, and when we got to the turnoff at Rishon Lezion, he said, "We're almost there, Yechiel." I started laughing. He looked at me inquiringly. "It's nothing... just reminded me of something," I said. He dropped me at the gate, I thanked him, and started walking to the barracks thinking 'there' must be the magical place I've heard of all my life.

I was almost 'there' when we walked in the fields at night from Russia to Germany. I was on Pop's shoulders and he would say, "We're almost there, Alec." When we drove in trucks from

Germany to Italy to board a ship going to Israel, my grandfather would tell me, "We are almost there, Alec." While sailing from Italy to Israel, I would wake up every morning asking my grandfather, "Are we there yet?" "Almost there," he would respond. The morning we stood together at the ship's railing, and he pointed to the land in our view, he said, "The Holy Land, Alec. We are almost there." When the British took us to Cypress instead, he cried and told me, "We were almost there... .we will be there soon." When the Haganah sneaked us out of Cypress and we landed in Lebanon by mistake, and had to walk at night, I held the hand of a young Israeli who kept telling me, "We are almost there, kid." When I ran away from home at 14 to live on the kibbutz, I used to listen to the young guys who had already served in the army. I made a calendar with the date, August 17, 1958 circled with an arrow pointing to that date, and wrote "17th Birthday—Almost There!" I started believing that 'There' was a magical place. A place where we all wanted to be.

I walked into the barracks and all of my guys were there with a "Welcome home, Yechi," and I thought this must be my 'There.'

Chapter 42

Hindsight is 20/20

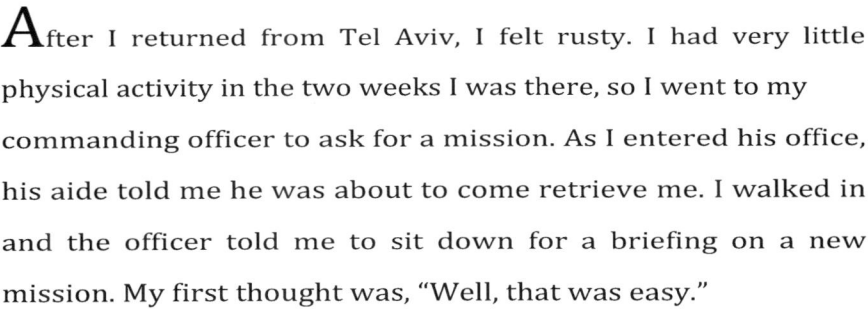

After I returned from Tel Aviv, I felt rusty. I had very little physical activity in the two weeks I was there, so I went to my commanding officer to ask for a mission. As I entered his office, his aide told me he was about to come retrieve me. I walked in and the officer told me to sit down for a briefing on a new mission. My first thought was, "Well, that was easy."

"Your friend, Meir, from Military Intelligence came by yesterday. They have intel that one of the Palestinian groups in Lebanon is planning a raid on Rosh Hanikra," he said. "We need to set up a welcoming party. Take two platoons, set up outside Rosh Hanikra, and stay for one week. If nothing happens, we will rotate... you'll come back and I'll send the other two platoons to replace you. Get your prep and briefing done today. Shoshana is coming for Shabbat dinner tonight. You'll take off at daybreak."

I was happy we would be seeing Shoshana Damari. She hadn't

sung to us for three weeks. Shoshana was an amazing singer, but more than that, she was part of our history. When you looked at her face, you could see traces of Arabia, North Africa, Spain and all the other places her ancestors had wandered before finding themselves back home in Israel. Shoshana didn't disappoint. It was good to be back with my guys, and after dinner Shoshana sang and joked with us for hours.

The next morning at 6 am, we took off from Tel Nof to Rosh Hanikra. Rosh Hanikra is a small town on a plateau on top of a mountain above Haifa. It is located on the border between Israel and Lebanon, on the coast of the Mediterranean Sea, and famous for its white chalk cliff face which opens up into spectacular grottos.

Lebanon used to be a pretty progressive country, but after our War of Independence, a lot of Palestinians settled there in refugee camps. They were not allowed to integrate into the country's society, and were kept in terrible conditions in tents with no running water or electricity. Unlike the Palestinian Arabs, the 850,000 Jews who were expelled from the Arab countries, came to Israel and were immediately integrated into Israeli society. The Palestinian camps became breeding grounds for terrorists. In the past year, terrorist activities had increased, mostly because of the training and weapons they were getting from the Arab countries.

We got to Rosh Hanikra on Saturday at 11 A.M. After erecting our tents outside the city, I met with my two platoon leaders, Tzveeka and Smolik. We walked up to the border fence to survey the two most likely locations to set up ambushes. We designated them "Area A" and "Area B." In addition to the three of us, I had eighteen men, for a total of twenty-one. We decided to rotate the men: seven men stayed to guard the campsite, seven to watch Area A, and seven to watch Area B. They were to set up at sunset and return to camp after daybreak.

The first two days were uneventful. On the third night, Smolik's unit was at Area A and my unit was at Area B. We arrived at our location after dark. It was a small elevated mound. As usual, we lay down in a circle approximately three feet apart so we had eyes on 360°. We usually took turns napping – every other man for two hours. I was up at 5 am. Just as the eastern sky turned copper where the sun crept over the horizon, I saw movement on the Lebanese side of the border fence. I touched the guy to my left to wake him. Within ten seconds, everyone was up and we re-formed our circle into an arc facing the border. I picked up the radio and clicked the button three times to alert Unit A. We watched as four terrorists cut the fence and crossed into Israel—all carrying AK-47 rifles. We allowed them to advance fifty yards. Then one of my men who spoke Arabic, ordered them to drop their guns and lay down, but they opened fire instead.

The firefight took about thirty seconds. We waited five minutes, then we got up. We knew they were dead, but we spread out and advanced carefully. It was very quiet. Suddenly, the man to my right tripped, and while falling, his finger triggered the Uzi he was carrying, emptying his magazine into some rocks to my right. Some of the shrapnel grazed my right hand.

There was no damage except for some bleeding from the cuts on my hand. We checked the terrorists and confirmed they were dead. I radioed the base and reported what had happened. I was told to secure the area and wait for my commanding officer, who was already on his way.

At 7:30 am, he arrived and I reported what had happened. He told his driver to take his jeep and me down to Rambam Hospital to get stitches. The hospital was at the bottom of the mountain we were on, at the outskirts of Haifa. I told Tzveeka to take command, got into the jeep, and we took off down the mountain.

In retrospect, I probably should have skipped the ride and walked.

Chapter 43

That Moment

―◆―

In life, there are clear cut beginnings... .those moments that split life into a "before" and an "after." Yet it is impossible, except in retrospect, to recognize the moment for what it is.

Five minutes after we took off for Haifa, the driver failed to negotiate a bend in the road, and the jeep flipped over the side, sliding into the canyon. Luckily, we hit a tree which broke our fall, probably saving our lives.

We crawled out of the jeep. I asked the driver if he was all right and he said he was. I felt OK but for my left knee, which was throbbing in pain. I found the radio, called Tzveeka and told him what had happened. Ten minutes later, he and five men righted the jeep, hooked it up to their truck, and pulled it up to the road. After a couple of tries, we actually got the jeep started and took off again for Haifa.

After finally arriving at the hospital, my hand was stitched up and x-rays of my knee were taken. The doctor told me he saw no breaks, but I should stay off my feet for a few days.

I called my commanding officer. After explaining to him what the doctor said, he approved my staying at my uncle's house in Haifa for a couple of days. My Uncle Zalman and Aunt Bronia lived in Bat Galim with their three children. It was about ten minutes from the hospital.

I was very close to my uncle, and after my family moved to the U.S., he had converted the porch in their house to a bedroom for me to stay in whenever I was there. I was dropped at their house about noon. Only my aunt and cousin Dubi (who was two years old) were home. My uncle was at work, and my cousins Mollie and Tzipi were at school. My aunt was duly upset when I limped in with my hand bandaged, but I told her it was just a minor injury. All I wanted to do was take the pain pills the doctor gave me and lie down. She replied, (like any Jewish mother would), "All right, but first you eat." She made me an omelet, I ate, then took the pills, and went to my room to lie down.

When I opened my eyes it was morning... I had slept the whole night! I jumped out of bed and fell on my face. The pain in my left leg was terrible. My knee was the size of a soccer ball, and I couldn't straighten my leg. I proceeded to slowly get dressed and hobbled to the kitchen where my uncle was having coffee. He took one look at me and said that he had better take me back to the hospital.

At the hospital, I saw the same doctor from the day before. He explained that the x-rays only showed bones and I must have torn some ligaments. This, he further explained, would put me out of commission for two to three months. I stayed in the hospital for a whole week, while the doctor made daily visits to straighten my leg, bit by bit. When the leg was finally straightened, he put a cast on it from my ankle to my groin, gave me crutches, and sent me to a rehabilitation facility on Mt. Carmel.

It was 1962 and medicine was surely not what it is today.

Chapter 44

Leaving

I checked into the rehabilitation hospital, was examined by a doctor and a physical therapist, and told that I would probably be there about 6 to 8 weeks – 3 to 4 weeks with the cast on, and the rest of the time in therapy. I was pissed off and depressed. The staff and the other injured soldiers were great, but I wanted to be back with my guys, doing my job.

After the week, I got used to the schedule: two hours of therapy after breakfast and two hours of therapy after lunch. The rest of the time I spent reading and playing games like shesh besh (backgammon), chess, or cards. Twice each week we were driven into town to the movies. I was lucky that all of my extended family lived in Haifa, and someone came to visit almost every day. Meir and Rivka visited often. Tzveeka, Ari and Smolik came whenever they could. Even so, time moved slowly.

After the second week, Sharon came and took me to lunch. He

said, "You know this would be a good time to go to university, like Rabin mentioned a while back." I told him I had been thinking that maybe I could go to America, where my parents and brothers lived, and attend university there. "That can be arranged. You will have to sign up to serve at least 2 years for every school year," he said. "Send the papers," I told him.

A week later, his aide came with the paperwork, and I signed it. After the cast was removed, the doctor told me I would need two more weeks of physical therapy. The next day, I had visitors: Rivka, Meir and Rafi Eitan. Rafi was Director of Operations for Mossad, and Rivka's boss. He explained that he came to talk about my trip to the United States.

"First of all, we want you to complete your studies without interruption. But in case of emergency, we may need your help. So while you are in Philadelphia, try to check in with our man at the Consulate. He has already spoken with Pennsylvania's Senator, Hugh Scott, asking him to expedite your student visa. Your parents already know you are coming. You leave in two weeks on a cruise ship owned by a Jewish company. During the cruise, you will be attending briefings with other officers like you. In Philadelphia, we have good relations with two universities – University of Pennsylvania and Temple. You will be able to register with either school. We also have Sayanim [Jews in other lands who help Israel] in Philadelphia, who are in business.

Our man at the Consulate will arrange for job interviews, if you need."

I just looked at him and said, "Can I shave by myself?" He laughed and said, "We will not use you unless we absolutely have to, and we are not allowed to operate in the U.S. anyway." "So when do I leave?" I asked. "Talk to Rivka," he replied. I looked at her and she said, "I will pick you up in two weeks and drive you down to the port in Haifa."

Rivka called early on a Thursday and told me she would be picking me up the next morning at 8 am. That day was very hard for me. Some of my family came to say goodbye. My Uncle Zalman said I looked sad. I admitted I was because I didn't want to leave. "But I'll be back," I said, hopefully.

After dinner, they all left. Tzveeka, Ari and Smolik came by with some of my belongings. We hung out for a few hours. Tzveeka and Smolik told me they weren't going to stay in the army. Instead, they were going to take off a year to travel and then start university. Ari said he liked being a jump instructor too much to leave.

After they left, I tried to go to sleep, but couldn't. Finally, at 4 am, I took a shower, got dressed, and went outside to lie down in the grass and watch the stars. I thought about all that had happened in my 21 years. Finally, when the stars disappeared, and the sky faded from blue to pink to orange, and the sun crested the trees, I returned to my room, picked up my kitbag, and went outside to wait for Rivka. She picked me up at 8 am. and within an hour, I boarded the ship in the port of Haifa. By noon we were on our way to New York City, U.S.A. I stayed on the deck, watching Israel recede until all I could see was water.

Chapter 45

Waterboarding

I went down to my cabin to unpack and saw the red light blinking on my phone. The message was to meet in Conference Room No. 3 at 3 pm. I got directions from the information counter and arrived on time.

There were seven people in the room – five young men about my age in chairs, and two middle-aged men standing in front of a blackboard. Introductions were made, and it turned out that the five of us were soldiers going to America on student visas. The men briefing us were from the Israeli Foreign Office – one stationed in New York, and one in Washington, D.C. They explained how important the U.S. was, and how large the Jewish community was. They gave us contact numbers for the embassies in the cities we were going to live, and told us to always remember that we were representing the State of Israel.

At 7 pm, we all met for dinner. After dinner, we split up and I went out on the deck, pulled up a lounge chair, and laid down.

The sky was full of stars and the sea was calm, but I wasn't. I just wasn't sure I had made the right decision. I missed Israel. I lit a cigarette and looked at the lighter with tears in my eyes. That lighter was and still is a beautifully engraved silver Ronson given to me by Yaki's grandmother, Esther, a week before I left. Yaki was my best friend who had been killed at Talfiq. The engraving

reads, "To Yechi from the Levin Family." It was, and is, my most cherished possession.

Finally, I decided that I made a decision and I must see it through. I went down to the game room and watched my new friends play pool. I played a few games of backgammon and decided to go to bed. It was after midnight before I finally fell asleep. I don't know how long I was out, but I awoke sweating, with my heart beating so fast it felt like it would jump out of my chest. I looked around and remembered I was on a ship. I don't know if it was being on the water that made me dream about waterboarding.

I was waterboarded once as a training exercise. It was horrible. I believe that waterboarding is torture, and shouldn't be allowed, but as officers we had to actually experience it. I went through it when I got my Captain's bars. The following is what I experienced:

I was led into a room by two sergeants. They proceeded to tie me to a chair. The chair was tilted back until my feet were off the ground. A towel was wrapped around my whole face and head. The room was silent, except for the sound of our breathing. Without warning, the first drops of cold water hit the towel. It sounded like raindrops hitting a tent. It stopped after a few seconds, the wetness spreading across my entire face. I tried to draw in a breath but couldn't. Panic doesn't adequately describe the feeling that set in. The water returned, hitting harder, flowing faster. I couldn't control my body's natural instinct to draw in air. I felt smothered, as if thrown into a pool of water while wrapped in plastic. I wanted to yell but couldn't, because I was choking, slowly dying. All I saw was blackness. Then, the towel was yanked off.

The light was blinding. I felt I was drowning. The chair was pushed forward and I spasmed, forcing the water out of my lungs. I coughed, spit up, vomited. The whole experience took ten seconds, but felt more like ten minutes.

That experience has haunted my sleep more than once since that day, and I would spend the rest of my life waking up in the same panic I felt that night on the ship.

Chapter 46

Coming to America

For the next two weeks, I stayed busy. I used the onboard gym and pool daily to stay in shape. We spent time in the recreation room playing games like backgammon, chess and cards while we continued to attend briefings by the two foreign office representatives.

Time went by so fast, that one morning I went up on deck for a run, but instead was struck by the site of the Statue of Liberty. Surely there is nothing more welcoming to a foreigner coming to America than the light of Lady Liberty's torch, and the inscribed poem by the Jewish poet, Emma Lazarus:

> Not like the brazen giant of Greek fame,
> With conquering limbs astride from land to land;
> Here at our sea-washed, sunset gates shall stand
> A mighty woman with a torch, whose flame
> Is the imprisoned lightning, and her name

Mother of Exiles. From her beacon-hand
Glows world-wide welcome; her mild eyes
command The air-bridged harbor that twin
cities frame. "Keep, ancient lands, your
storied pomp!" cries she With silent lips.
"Give me your tired, your poor, Your
huddled masses yearning to breathe free,
The wretched refuse of your teeming shore.
Send these, the homeless, tempest-tost to me, I
lift my lamp beside the golden door!

The foreign office men had taken care of all the paperwork and customs forms. By noon, I walked outside the terminal and saw Pop and my mother waving. I hadn't seen them in three years. Pop hugged and kissed me. I was very happy to see him, but even as my mother hugged and kissed me, all of the old feelings came back – hurt, betrayal and anger. I realized that, in my life, I never had a tender moment with her – no hugs, no kisses, even when I was little. She never wiped my tears when I hurt myself like my aunts did, never told me she loved me, and I don't remember telling her I loved her either. Actually, I don't remember ever feeling love for her.

When she hugged me on arrival in New York, all I could think about was why Pop hadn't left her after all the times she embarrassed and betrayed him. I felt really bad for him. I was anxious to see my brothers, so I hugged her back, put my kitbag in the trunk, and we took off for Philadelphia. Pop said it would take two to three hours to get there.

At 4 pm, we pulled in front of a row house and I saw three big guys sitting on the steps. It took me a while to realize that these were my brothers. Our reunion was happy and loud. We hugged and kissed and jumped around and made so much noise that the neighbors came out to investigate. Those who knew what was going on applauded and yelled "Baruch Haba, Alec!", which is a Hebrew welcome.

I was really happy to see my brothers. Shaya was very big – just like Pop both in size and mannerisms. Ben was also big and looked like Pop, but a bit more reserved. Ezra was still a little kid and didn't look like anyone in the family, but he was the most emotional, laughing and talking a lot. He hung onto me, telling me with unbridled enthusiasm that I was to sleep in his room. He was (and still is) a little fire plug.

The reunion with my brothers was more emotional than I ever expected. I realized how much I loved and missed them. We went into the house, put my kitbag in Ezra's room and went downstairs where Pop had an open bottle of vodka. He poured some for me and himself. My mother had some wine, and my brothers had something called "Mountain Dew." Pop said, "Welcome home Alec... .L'chaim." Everyone drank.

I looked around thinking, "This is America." And wondered what's next.

Chapter 47

Nightmare #1

I'm standing in the town square of a small village. I know it's in the Middle East, but it's not home, like Haifa where I used to live as a child. Neither is it Neve Eitan, the kibbutz where I grew up as a young man before enlisting in the IDF. Not home, Israel, the land I love. The place I would defend with my life.

The harsh glare of the sun is blinding and it bears down on a mosque in the distance. It reflects off its gilded dome, making my eyes squint. It beats down on my neck, making me sweat. My eyes adjust from the glare and I look down. I'm in uniform: helmet, leather boots, and fatigues. I feel the weight of my pack on my shoulders. I'm alone. Not just alone, but exposed, standing out in the open in the middle of the square.

I scan the village: stucco walls pockmarked with small arms fire, structures reduced to rubble by artillery rounds. The smell tells me that the damage is recent.

I reach for my weapon, but I have no Uzi, no sidearm... no nothing. "This isn't right," I think. "I shouldn't be here like this, unarmed, out in the open. I am a lieutenant in the I.D.F. in charge of eight other recon paratroopers... wolves, lean killing soldiers at the top of the spear."

I call out their names... nothing. Where the hell are my guys?
In the middle of the square is a dead Israeli soldier. I can't see his face, but I know he is one of mine. He's on his back. He's taken a direct hit to the stomach.

His intestines have spilled out and chickens are pecking at them.

Chapter 48

What is a Hero?

I wake up soaking wet in a dark room. I look at my watch. It says "4:30." Where am I? Then I hear someone breathing nearby. I look over towards the sound and see another bed. I walk over. It's my little brother, Ezra. It all comes back to me. I'm in America, in my parents house in Philadelphia, Pennsylvania. I was dreaming.

I've been having these dreams for years. I dream of Yaki's death. I dream of my throat being cut by Arab marauders at age 16. I dream of a sniper's bullet that takes my buddy's head off, while standing next to me at the latrine. I dream of the 5-year-old daughter of my swimming coach shot in the head by terrorists.

I put on my shorts, t-shirt and sneakers, and go for a run. I wonder how I can deal with my brothers. They have an image of me being like Superman. My brother Shaya wants me to go talk to his boss at the bakery where he works part time. My brother

Ezra, wants me to go to his school and beat up some older kids who are bullying him and his friends. Meanwhile, I'm having nightmares, waking up sweating and shaking.

How do I explain to them that I was afraid before every parachute jump? And, that I cried when my friends were killed? Or, that I was devastated, along with my buddies, when our adopted dog died from a snake bite? How do I explain to my brothers, that like most of the men I served with, I have bad dreams tormenting me?

When I got back, everyone was up, so I grabbed a quick shower before we sat down for breakfast. As usual, my little brother talked. He told us that at Hebrew school on Sunday, the kids talked about the Israeli army, especially about the Paratroopers. To them they are heroes, like Superman. I looked up and said, "Superman is not a hero." The room fell silent, and everyone looked at me.

"Let me give you an example. An old man is walking down the street, and suddenly a gang of hoodlums attack him with baseball bats and knives. But before they can hurt him, Superman jumps in and saves him."

"OK," says Ezra. "You can see he is a hero."

"Right," I respond. "Then let me give you another example. An old man is walking down the street, and suddenly a gang of hoodlums attack him like before. But another man walking to work sees what's happening and jumps in to help. So who is the hero, Ezra? Superman, who risks nothing, or the average man who risks everything – even his life, to help another?"

Ezra is quiet for a moment, then says, "I'm going to tell this to the kids in Sunday school."

> "Courage is not the absence of fear, but the triumph over it. The brave man is not he who is not afraid, but he who conquers that fear." — Nelson Mandella

Chapter 49

My Mother's House

On Monday morning, Pop drove me downtown to the Israeli Consulate where I met with Natan, the Cultural Attaché. That was his title, but he really worked for Rafi Eitan, Israel's Director of Operations for Mossad. Natan was young, maybe 30, and in good shape, so the first thing I asked was where had he served. He replied that he had spent two years in the paratroopers, then military intelligence, and now Mossad. After this introduction, he got down to the business at hand.

"I have your folder," he said, "so I know who you are and why you are here. As I see it, your priorities are to one, learn English; two, to get a driver's license; and, three, to get a job." He handed me a sheet of paper, with addresses and phone numbers of contacts for each of these tasks.

The last contact, the one for a job, was for the Levy family, who had demonstrated a love for Israel. It turned out that their son,

Marvin, was my age and spent a few months in a kibbutz, had some knowledge of the Hebrew language, and was anxious to meet me.

The fourth priority mentioned by Natan was to check in with him at least once a week. When we were done with our business, I walked him out to the waiting room to meet Pop. They talked for a few minutes before Natan asked if there was anything else I needed. "Yes," I said. "I would like to visit Princeton University to see the place where Einstein worked and taught." He responded with some surprise, then offered that it was something he had always wanted to do as well. He arranged to pick me up on Saturday morning and take me himself.

On our way back to my parents' house, Pop and I stopped for lunch. We had the longest discussion ever in my life. It felt great. But, when we got home, my mother started hollering at Pop about how she does all the work and all the thinking in the family because "he is just not smart." It was embarrassing. I went outside, walked over to the park and sat on a bench watching kids play soccer.

As I sat, I remembered something from Homer's masterpiece, "The Odyssey." When Odysseus returns home unrecognized as a beggar, his son cannot sit quiet as his mother refuses to accept that her husband has returned:

"Cruel mother, you with your hard heart!

Why do you spurn my father so?

Why don't you sit beside him?

Engage him, ask him questions?

What other wife could have a spirit so unbending?

Your heart was always harder than a rock!"

These were my thoughts during my first days in America. Inevitably, I came to wonder why I was here. Israel is my home. I am somebody in Israel. In Israel, I am everything I ever dreamed of being. I love my country, and I love my people.

Right then, one of the kids scored a goal and the rest of his team ran over to him, slapping his back, hugging and giving him high-fives. I looked at their happy faces and decided I would give it 3 months. If I was unable to move out of the mother's house by then, I would go back home to start my education at Haifa University.

Epilogue

America brought me to my final name. This was the name given to me by my cousin Shelley, who insisted that we all become "Americanized." My brother Shaya became Steve, Ezra became Eric, and I became Allen, a name I still feel doesn't suit me. Many in my family still call me Alec.

I did, in fact, get out of my mother's house. After three months at University of Pennsylvania, I learned enough English to get by, got my driver's license, and worked in the warehouse of Majestic Penn State. Marvin Levy, the son of the owner, became a good friend and introduced me to his friends. One of them was a single mother named Gloria. We started dating.

By the end of three months, Natan found a better job for me at Keystone Roofing, another Jewish owned company. The owner took a liking to me, and arranged for me to enroll at Temple University to study architectural and building design. Within a year, I became the operations manager for the company.

I married Gloria that year and bought a house. My desire to leave my mother's house was fierce, so marrying Gloria was my way out. Though the marriage ended in divorce nine years later, we had two wonderful children, Lynne and Ken. Tragically, Lynne's life was cut short by pancreatic cancer – a loss I suffer to this day. Ken married, then divorced, and gave me a beautiful granddaughter named Farrah.

After my divorce from Gloria, I married another single mother, Rita. The marriage didn't last very long, but I remained close with one of her daughters, Debbie, who is still in daily contact with me.

During my 19 years in Philadelphia, I never finished college and my dream of becoming a general in the IDF was derailed. Nevertheless, throughout my time there I remained in touch with the Israeli Consulate. In 1965, I participated in a mission for Israel with my friend Rivka. In 1967, the Six Day War broke out. I rushed to the Consulate but never made it to Israel. In 1973, the Yom Kippur War began and I dropped everything to have my brother, Eric, give me a ride to Kennedy Airport. I got to Israel on the third day of the war. On the fifth day I joined my brigade at the Suez Canal under the command of Arik Sharon. It was a terrible battle unlike anything I had experienced with my old recon unit. I saw things no one should ever have to see. After the war I came back to Philadelphia with a brain full of terrible scenes.

In 1979, Gloria took our 2 children and moved to California. I followed in order to be able to stay in contact with them. I got a job as Operations Manager at a very large roofing company. In 1980, they asked me to open a new branch of the company in San Diego, a position I accepted.

After moving to San Diego, I drove up to the Los Angeles area nearly every weekend to visit my old friends from Philadelphia, Sherre and Irv. One weekend, Sherre set me up on a blind date. I remember walking into their kitchen and seeing a young, beautiful woman named Pia standing on a chair, reaching for a bottle of wine in the upper cabinet. I fell for her immediately and, for the first time in my life, I found true love.

We married in 1981 and I immediately adopted her 4-year-old son, Michaelis. Pia's parents, Phil and Julia, embraced me completely. I became very close to Pia's father, who was the kindest, smartest and most unassuming person I ever met. I finally had the father I had been looking for all of my life.

Left to right: Julia, Molly (cousin from New Jersey), Michaelis, Phil, Pia, Allen

Still working in the roofing business, I decided to try consulting and just happened upon my first client on a roof at a large shopping mall. Pia and I wound up opening up a very successful roofing consulting office with clients all over the U.S. and Canada. The business was bought out by another firm in 2000 and I retired shortly thereafter.

Michaelis gave us two grandsons, Misha and Jai, with whom we are close, along with their mothers, whom we consider our daughters.

My Name Was Alec. A Memoir by Allen Jacoby

As of this writing, Pia and I have been together for 39 years and are still very much in love. At the age of 77, I decided to write this book to try to figure out who I really am:

    I am a soldier,

    A brother, father and a son,

    A husband and a grandfather,

    A refugee and a patriot,

    A cynic and an idealist;

    A student of history

    And a defender of the Jewish people.

I never returned to live in Israel.

Made in the USA
Monee, IL
24 May 2020